THE NEW DARE TO DISCIPLINE

Since *Dare to Discipline* was originally published, Dr Dobson has served three American presidents in various responsibilities. These include appointments to the National Advisory Commission to the Office of Juvenile Justice and Delinquency Prevention, the Attorney General's Commission on Pornography, Health and Human Services' Teen Pregnancy Prevention Panel, the Attorney General's Board on Missing and Exploited Children, and various other governmental assignments. He was also appointed chairman of the US Army Family Initiative by then chief of staff of the army, General John Wickham. In 1987, Dr Dobson was awarded the designation 'The Children's Friend' by Child Help USA, the leading opponent of child abuse in the United States.

Dr Dobson holds a PhD in child development from the university of Southern California and five honorary doctorates from Pepperdine University, Franciscan University in Steubenville, Seattle Pacific University, Asbury Seminary, and Mid-America Nazarene College. He is the father of two grown children and resides in Colorado Springs with his wife of thirty-three years, Shirley.

By the same author:
The Strong-Willed Child
(Discipline While You Can)
Preparing for Adolescence
Man to Man About Women
Love Must Be Tough
Dr Dobson Answers Your Questions

The New
Dare to Discipline

DR JAMES DOBSON

KINGSWAY PUBLICATIONS
EASTBOURNE

Biblical quotations are taken from the following:
NIV—the New International Version © 1973, 1978, 1984
by the International Bible Society.
RSV—the Revised Standard Version © 1946, 1952, 1971, 1973,
the Division of Education and Ministry of the National
Council of the Churches of Christ in the USA.
KJV—King James Version, Crown copyright.
PHILLIPS—The New Testament in Modern English
by J.B. Phillips, © J.B. Phillips 1958, 1960, 1972.

Co-published in South Africa with SCB Publishers
Cornelis Struik House, 80 McKenzie Street
Cape Town 8001, South Africa
Reg no 04/02203/06

ISBN 0 85476 803 3

Designed and produced by Bookprint Creative Services
P.O. Box 827, BN21 3YJ, England for
KINGSWAY PUBLICATIONS
Lottbridge Drove, Eastbourne, E. Sussex, BN23 6NT.
Printed in Great Britain.

To Danae, Ryan, and their mother Shirley,
I affectionately dedicate the pages of this book
and the remaining years of my life.

*(Written initially in 1971,
and reconfirmed more than two decades later!)*

Contents

1

The Challenge

This is a book about children and those who love them. The first edition was written in the early seventies when I was a professor of pediatrics at the University of Southern California School of Medicine. Our own children were still preschoolers, which made it risky to offer advice about parenting techniques. That's like a manager bragging in the first half about how he expects to win the game. Nevertheless, I had seen enough academically and professionally to have developed some firm convictions about how children should be brought up and what they needed from their parents.

More than twenty years and two million copies of *Dare to Discipline* have come and gone since I first sat down to write. That passage of time has broadened my horizon and, hopefully, sharpened my vision. I've worked with thousands of families and I've considered the child-rearing views of many authorities and colleagues. My children have paddled through adolescence and have established homes of their own. Thus, it is a special privilege for me to turn back the clock now and revisit the themes with which I first grappled so many years ago.

One might expect my views of child development and parenting to have evolved significantly within the intervening years. Such is not the case. Admittedly, the social backdrop for the original *Dare to Discipline* has changed dramatically, which is why this book needed to be revised and expanded. The student revolution that raged through the late sixties and early seventies has subsided. Woodstock and the Vietnam War are distant memories, and university campuses are again quieter and less rebellious. But children haven't changed, nor will they ever. I'm even more convinced now that the principles of good parenting are eternal, having originated with the Creator of families. The inspired concepts in Scripture have been handed down generation after generation and are just as valid for the twenty-first century as they were for our ancestors. Unfortunately, many of today's parents have never heard those time-honoured ideas and have no clue about what they're trying to accomplish at home.

I'll never forget a mother in that predicament who asked for my help in handling her defiant three-year-old daughter, Sandy. She realised that her tiny little girl had hopelessly beaten her in a contest of wills, and the child had become a tyrant and a dictator. On the afternoon prior to our conversation, an incident occurred which was typical of Sandy's way of doing business. The mother (I'll call her Mrs Nichols) put the youngster down for a nap, but knew it was unlikely she would stay in bed. Sandy was not accustomed to doing anything she didn't fancy, and naptime was not on her list of fun things to do in the afternoon.

On this occasion, however, the child was more interested in antagonising her mother than in merely having her own way. Sandy began to scream. She yelled loudly enough to upset the whole neighbourhood, fraying Mrs Nichols' jangled nerves. Then she tearfully demanded various things, including a glass of water.

At first Mrs Nichols refused to comply with the orders, but she surrendered when Sandy's screaming again reached a peak of intensity. As the glass of water was delivered, the mischievous child pushed it aside, refusing to drink because her mother had not brought it soon enough. Mrs Nichols stood offering the water for a few minutes, then said she would take it back to the kitchen if Sandy did not drink by the time she counted to five.

Sandy set her jaw and waited through the count: 'three . . . four . . . five!' As Mrs Nichols grasped the glass and walked towards the kitchen, the child screamed for the water. Sandy dangled her harassed mother back and forth like a yo-yo until she tired of the sport.

Mrs Nichols and her little daughter are among the many casualties of an unworkable, illogical philosophy of child management which has long dominated the literature on this subject. This mother had read that a child will eventually respond to reason and forbearance, ruling out the need for firm leadership. She had been told to encourage the child's rebellion because it offered a valuable release of hostility. She attempted to implement the recommendations of the experts who suggested that she verbalise the child's feelings in a moment of conflict: 'You want the water but you're angry because I brought it too late' . . . 'You don't want me to take the water back to the kitchen' . . . 'You don't like me because I make you take naps.' She had also been taught that conflicts between parent and child were to be perceived as misunderstandings or differences in viewpoint.

Unfortunately, Mrs Nichols and her advisors were wrong! She and her child were involved in no simple difference of opinion: she was being challenged, mocked and defied by her daughter. No heart-to-heart talk would resolve this nose-to-nose confrontation, because the real issue was totally unrelated to water or the nap or other aspects of the particular circumstances. The actual meaning behind this conflict and a hundred others was simply this: Sandy was brazenly rejecting the authority of her mother. The way Mrs Nichols handled these confrontations would determine the nature of their future relationship, especially during the adolescent years.

Much has been written about the dangers of harsh, oppressive, unloving discipline; these warnings are valid and should be heeded. However, the consequences of oppressive discipline have been cited as justification for the abdication of leadership. That is foolish. There are times when a strong-willed child will clench his little fists and dare his parents to accept his challenges. He is not motivated by frustration or inner hostility, as it is often supposed. He merely wants to know where the boundaries lie and who's available to enforce them.

Many well-meaning specialists have waved the banner of tolerance, but offered no solution for defiance. They have stressed the importance of parental understanding of the child, and I concur. But we need to teach children that they have a few things to learn about their parents, too!

Mrs Nichols and all her contemporaries need to know

how to set limits, and what to do when defiant behaviour occurs. This disciplinary activity must take place within the framework of love and affection, which is often difficult for parents who view these roles as contradictory. *The New Dare to Discipline* is addressed, in part, to this vital aspect of bringing up healthy, respectful, happy children.

The term 'discipline' is not limited to the context of confrontation, and neither is this book. Children also need to be taught *self*-discipline and responsible behaviour. They need assistance in learning how to handle the challenges and obligations of living. They must learn the art of self-control. They should be equipped with the personal strength needed to meet the demands imposed on them by their school, peer group, and later adult responsibilities.

There are those who believe these characteristics cannot be taught—that the best we can do is send children down the path of least resistance, sweeping aside the hurdles during their formative years. The advocates of this laissez-faire philosophy would recommend that youngsters be allowed to fail in school if they choose . . . or maintain their bedrooms like proverbial pigsties . . . or let their puppies go hungry.

I reject this notion and have accumulated considerable evidence to refute it. Children thrive best in an atmosphere of genuine love, undergirded by reasonable, consistent discipline. In a day of widespread drug usage, immorality, sexually transmitted diseases, vandalism and violence, we must not depend on hope and luck to fashion the critical attitudes we value in our children. Permissiveness has not simply failed as an approach to child rearing. It's been a disaster for those who have tried it.

When properly applied, loving discipline works! It stimulates tender affection, made possible by *mutual* respect between a parent and child. It bridges the gap which otherwise separates family members who should love and trust each other. It allows the God of our ancestors to be introduced to our beloved children. It permits teachers to do the kind of job in classrooms for which they are commissioned. It encourages a child to respect other people and live as a responsible, constructive citizen.

As might be expected, there is a price tag on these benefits: they require courage, consistency, conviction, diligence and enthusiastic effort. In short, one must *dare to discipline* in an environment of unmitigated love. We'll discuss the methods by which that can be accomplished in subsequent chapters.

2

Common Sense and Your Child

Methods and philosophies of discipline have been the subject of heated debate and disagreement throughout the past seventy years. Psychologists and pediatricians and university professors have all got in on the act, telling parents how to bring up their children properly. Unfortunately, many of these 'experts' have been in direct contradiction with one another, spreading more heat than light about a subject of great importance.

Perhaps that is why the pendulum has swung back and forth regularly between harsh, oppressive control and the unstructured permissiveness we saw in the mid-twentieth century. It is time we realised that *both* extremes leave their characteristic scars on the lives of young victims, and I would be hard pressed to say which is more damaging.

At the oppressive end of the continuum, a child suffers the humiliation of total domination. The atmosphere is icy and rigid, and he lives in constant fear. He is unable to make his own decisions, and his personality is squelched beneath the hobnailed boot of parental authority.

15

Lasting characteristics of dependency; deep, abiding anger; and even psychosis can emerge from this persistent dominance.

Of greater concern are the boys and girls who are being subjected to physical and emotional abuse. There are millions of families out there in which these unthinkable crimes are being committed day after day. It is hard to believe just how cruel some mothers and fathers can be to a defenceless, wide-eyed child who doesn't understand why he or she is hated. The cases I've dealt with over the years—of unloved and abused children—are impossible to forget. I remember the terrible father who regularly wrapped his small son's head in the sheet that the boy had wet the night before. Then he crammed the tot upside down into the toilet bowl for punishment. I also think of the disturbed mother who cut out her child's eyes with a razor blade. That poor little girl will go through life blind, knowing that her own mother deprived her of sight! Horrible acts like these are now occurring every day in cities and towns around us.

We should also recognise that there are many ways to abuse a child without breaking the law. It can be done subtly by ignoring a boy or girl's desperate need to be nurtured. It can be accomplished by unjust and unfair punishment, including parental acts that might pass for 'corporal punishment'—such as routinely hitting, slapping, kicking, and throwing the child to the ground. Then there is the entire range of humiliating behaviour by a mother or father, making a youngster feel stupid and weird and unloved. Within certain limits, these behaviours are not illegal. There is no one to rescue the pitiful child who is being twisted and warped by the big people around him. Let *nothing* in this book ever hint at my approval of such tyranny.

Let me say again with the strongest emphasis that aggressive, hard-nosed, 'Mummy Dearest' kinds of discipline are destructive to children and must not be tolerated. Parents who are cold and stern with their sons and daughters often leave them damaged for life. I could easily be misunderstood at this point, having written this book in which I recommend (in Chapter 4) the judicious use of corporal punishment under specific circumstances and limits. May all doubts be dispelled. *I don't believe in parental harshness.* End of story. Children are incredibly vulnerable to rejection, ridicule, criticism and anger at home, and they deserve to grow up in an environment of safety, acceptance and warmth.

We must acknowledge, as indicated earlier, that the opposite extreme is also damaging to children. In the absence of adult leadership, the child is his own master from his earliest babyhood. He thinks the world revolves around his heady empire, and he often has utter contempt and disrespect for those closest to him. Anarchy and chaos reign in his home, and his mother is often the most nervous, frustrated woman in her street. When the child is young, the mother is stranded at home because she is too embarrassed to take her little spitfire anywhere. It would be worth the hardships she endures if this condition produced healthy, secure children. It clearly does not.

Many of the writers offering their opinions on the subject of discipline in recent years have confused parents, stripping them of the ability to lead in their own homes. They have failed to acknowledge the desire of most youngsters to rule their own lives and prevail in the contest of wills that typically occurs between generations.

In my book *The Strong-Willed Child (Discipline While You Can)* I quoted from a text on parenting entitled, *Your Child from Two to Five,* published during the permissive 1950s. In it was a bit of advice paraphrased from the writings of a Dr Luther Woodward, as follows:

> What do you do when your preschooler calls you a 'big stinker' or threatens to flush you down the toilet? Do you scold . . . punish . . . or sensibly take it in your stride? Dr. Woodward recommends a positive policy of understanding as the best and fastest way to help a child outgrow this verbal violence. When parents fully realize that all little tots feel angry and destructive at times, they are better able to minimize these outbursts. Once the preschooler gets rid of his hostility, the desire to destroy is gone and instinctive feelings of love and affection have a chance to sprout and grow. Once the child is six or seven, parents can rightly let the child know that he is expected to be outgrowing sassing his parents.[1]

Having offered that sage advice, with which I disagree strongly, Dr Woodward then told parents to brace themselves for unjust criticism. He wrote, 'But this policy [of letting children engage in defiance] takes a broad perspective and a lot of composure, especially when friends and relatives voice disapproval and warn that you are bringing up a brat.'

In this case, your friends and relatives will probably be right. Dr Woodward's recommendation is typical of the advice given to parents in the mid-twentieth century. It encourages them to stand passively through the formative years when respect for authority can so easily be taught. I responded to that counsel this way in *The Strong-Willed Child:*

> Dr. Woodward's suggestion is based on the simplistic notion that children will develop sweet and loving attitudes if we adults will permit and encourage their temper tantrums during childhood. According to the optimistic Dr. Woodward, the tot who has been calling his mother a 'big stinker' for six or seven years can be expected to embrace her suddenly in love and dignity. That outcome is most improbable. Dr. Woodward's creative 'policy of understanding' (which means stand and do nothing) offers a one-way ticket to adolescent rebellion in many cases.[2]

I believe that if it is desirable for children to be kind, appreciative and pleasant, those qualities should be taught— not hoped for. If we want to see honesty, truthfulness and unselfishness in our offspring, then these characteristics should be the conscious objectives of our early instructional process. If it is important to produce respectful, responsible young citizens, then we should set out to mould them accordingly. The point is obvious: *heredity does not equip a child with proper attitudes; children learn what they are taught.* We cannot expect the coveted behaviour to appear magically if we have not done our early homework.

The kind of advice Dr Woodward and others have offered to mothers and fathers through the years has led to a type of paralysis in dealing with their children. In the absence of 'permission' to step in and lead, parents were left with only their anger and frustration in response to defiant behaviour.

That thought immediately brings to mind a family I knew with four of the most unruly children I had ever

met. These youngsters were the terrors of their neighbourhood. They were disrespectful, loud and aggressive.
They roamed in and out of other people's garages,
helping themselves to tools and equipment. It became
necessary for neighbours to remove the tops from outside
taps, because these children enjoyed leaving the water
running when the families were out.

It was interesting to observe the method of discipline
used by their mother, if only because it provided a mem-
orable example of what didn't work. Her system of controlling her brood boiled down to a simple formula.
When they became too noisy or cantankerous in the
garden, she would rush out of the door about once every
hour and scream, 'I have had it with you kids! I have just
had it with you!' Then she would turn and go back into
the house. The children never even glanced up at her. If
they knew she was there they gave no indication of it. But
she apparently felt it was sufficient to burst out of the
door like a cuckoo clock every so often and remind them
she was still around. There must be a better way to handle
the awesome task of parenting that God has assigned to
us.

If both extremes are harmful, how do we find the safety
of the middle ground? Surely, there is a logical, reasonable philosophy of child rearing that will guide our
day-by-day interactions at home. Can't the social scien-
tists come up with a workable game plan? Perhaps this
will sound like heresy coming from a man who spent ten
years of his life in behavioural and medical research, but
I don't believe the scientific community is the best source
of information on proper parenting techniques. There
have been some worthwhile studies, to be sure. But the

subject of parent-child interactions is incredibly complex and subtle. The only way to investigate it scientifically is to reduce the relationship to its simplest common denominators, so it can be examined. But in so doing, the overall tone is missed. Some things in life are so complicated that they almost defy rigorous scrutiny, and parental discipline (in my view) appears to be one of them.

The best source of guidance for parents can be found in the wisdom of the Judeo-Christian ethic, which originated with the Creator and was then handed down generation by generation from the time of Christ. This is what my mother, my grandmother, and my great-grandmother understood almost intuitively. There was within Western culture a common knowledge about children and their needs. Not everyone applied it, but most people agreed with its tenets. When a new baby was born 100 years ago, aunts and sisters and grandmothers came over to teach the new mother how to care for her infant. What they were doing was passing along the traditional wisdom . . . the heritage . . . to the next generation, which would later perform the same service for those who had just become mothers. That system worked pretty well until the 1920s and thereafter. Slowly, the culture began to lose confidence in that tradition and shifted its allegiance to the experts. Behaviourist J.B. Watson was one of the first and most influential gurus to come along. He offered what he called a 'foolproof' method of child rearing, and mothers bought it hook, line and sinker. If only they would follow his advice, he said, they could produce any kind of child they wanted . . . 'a doctor, lawyer, artist, merchant-chief, and—yes—even a beggar-man and a thief'.

Watson advised parents, if they wanted the best results, to show no affection for their offspring. He wrote:

> Never hug and kiss them, never let them sit on your lap. If you must, kiss them once on the forehead when they say good night. Shake hands with them in the morning. . . .
>
> Remember when you are tempted to pet your child, that mother love is a dangerous instrument. An instrument which may inflict a never-healing wound, a wound which may make infancy unhappy, adolescence a nightmare, an instrument which may wreck your adult son or daughter's vocational future and their chances for marital happiness.[3]

This advice from Dr Watson comes across today like pure nonsense, and indeed, that's just what it is. In fact, it's difficult to believe anyone gave credibility to such advice even in 1928. Yet Watson was enormously popular in his day, and his books sold in the millions. Mothers and fathers worked diligently to 'condition' their children in the way recommended by this half-baked hot dog.

Then came Dr Sigmund Freud, and Dr Benjamin Spock, and Dr A. S. Neill (see Chapter 7), and Dr Tom Gordon, and Dr Ruth Westheimer, and Phil Donahue, and Oprah Winfrey, and magazines such as *Cosmopolitan,* and finally, a newspaper for 'enquiring minds who want to know'. With every new, off-the-wall suggestion that came along, I asked myself: If their new approach to child rearing is so wonderful, why was it not observed until now? How come 20,000 million parents across more than 5,000 years failed to notice the concept? Certainly, the accumulated experience of all that mothering and fathering should count for *something*!

My primary purpose in writing this book, both the

1970 version and this recomposition, has been to record for posterity my understanding of the Judeo-Christian concept of parenting that has guided millions of mothers and fathers for centuries. I am convinced that it will prove successful in *your* home, too. Let's move on, then, to examine five underpinnings to commonsense child rearing.

Respect for parents

Developing respect for parents is the critical factor in child management. It is imperative that a child learns to respect his parents—not to satisfy their egos, but because his relationship with them provides the basis for his later attitude towards all other people. His early view of parental authority becomes the cornerstone of his future outlook on school authority, law enforcement officers, employers, and others with whom he will eventually live and work. The parent-child relationship is the first and most important social interaction a youngster will have, and the flaws and knots experienced there can often be seen later in life.

Respect for parents must be maintained for another equally important reason. If you want your child to accept your values when he reaches his teen years, then you must be worthy of his respect during his younger days. When a child can successfully defy his parents during his first fifteen years, laughing in their faces and stubbornly flaunting his authority, he develops a natural contempt for them.

'Stupid old Mum and Dad! I have them wound around my little finger. Of course they love me, but I really think they're afraid of me.' A child may not utter these words, but he feels them each time he outsmarts his elders and wins the confrontations and battles. Later he is likely to demonstrate his disrespect in a more blatant manner. Viewing his parents as being unworthy of his respect, he may very well reject every vestige of their philosophy and faith.

This factor is also of vital importance to Christian parents who wish to transmit their love for Jesus Christ to their sons and daughters. Why? Because young children typically identify their parents—and especially their fathers—with God. Therefore, if Mum and Dad are not worthy of respect, then neither are their morals, their country, their values and beliefs, or even their religious faith.

I was shocked to see this close identification between God and me in the mind of our son when he was two years old. Ryan had watched his mother and me pray before we ate each meal, but he had never been asked to say grace. One day when I was away on a business trip, Shirley spontaneously turned to the toddler and asked if he would like to pray before they ate. The invitation startled him, but he folded his little hands, bowed his head, and said, 'I love you, Daddy. Amen.'

When I returned home and Shirley told me what had happened, the story unsettled me. I hadn't realised the degree to which Ryan linked me with his 'heavenly Father'. I wasn't even sure I wanted to stand in those shoes. It was too big a job, and I didn't want the responsibility. But I had no choice; nor do you. God has given us the task of representing him during the formative years of parenting. That's why it is so critically important for us to acquaint our kids with God's two predominant natures: his unfathomable love and his justice. If we love our children but permit them to treat us disrespectfully and with disdain, we have distorted their understanding of the Father. On the other hand, if we are rigid disciplinarians who show no love, we have tipped the scales in the other direction. What we teach our children about the Lord is a function, to some degree, of how we model love and discipline in our relationship with them. Scary, huh?

The issue of respect is also useful in guiding parents' interpretation of given behaviour. First, they should decide whether an undesirable act represents a direct challenge to their authority . . . to their leadership position as the father or mother. The form of disciplinary action they take should depend on the result of that evaluation.

For example, suppose little Chris is acting silly in the living room and falls into a table, breaking many expensive china cups and other trinkets. Or suppose Wendy loses her bicycle or leaves her mother's coffeepot out in the rain. These are acts of childish irresponsibility and should be handled as such. Perhaps the parent will ignore the event or maybe have the child work to pay for the losses—depending on his age and maturity, of course.

However, these examples do not constitute direct challenges to authority. They do not emanate from wilful, haughty disobedience and therefore should not result in serious discipline. In my opinion, spankings (which we will discuss later) should be reserved for the moment a child (between the age of eighteen months to ten years old) expresses to parents a defiant 'I will not!' or 'You shut up!' When youngsters convey this kind of stiff-necked rebellion, you must be willing to respond to the challenge immediately. When nose-to-nose confrontation occurs between you and your child, it is not the time to discuss the virtues of obedience. It is not the occasion to send him to his room to pout. Nor is it appropriate to postpone disciplinary measures until your tired spouse plods home from work.

You have drawn a line in the dirt, and the child has deliberately flopped his little pink toe across it. Who is going to win? Who has the most courage? Who is in charge here? If you do not conclusively answer these questions for your strong-willed children, they will precipitate other battles designed to ask them again and again. It is the ultimate paradox of childhood that youngsters want to be led, but insist that their parents earn the right to lead them.

When mothers and fathers fail to take charge in moments of challenge, they create for themselves and their families a potential lifetime of heartache. That's what happened in the case of the Holloways, who were the parents of a teenager named Becky (not their real names). Mr Holloway came to see me in desperation one afternoon and related the cause for his concern. Becky had never been required to obey or respect her parents, and her early years were a strain on the entire family. Mrs Holloway was confident Becky would eventually become more manageable, but that never happened. She held her parents in utter contempt from her youngest childhood and was sullen, disrespectful, selfish and unco-operative. Mr and Mrs Holloway did not feel they had the right to make demands on their daughter, so they smiled politely and pretended not to notice her horrid behaviour.

Their magnanimous attitude became more difficult to

maintain as Becky steamrolled into puberty and adolescence. She was a perpetual malcontent, sneering at her family in disgust. Mr and Mrs Holloway were afraid to antagonise her in any way because she would throw the most violent tantrums imaginable. They were victims of emotional blackmail. They thought they could buy her co-operation, which led them to install a private telephone in her room. She accepted it without gratitude and accumulated a staggering bill during the first month of usage.

They thought a party might make her happy, and Mrs Holloway worked very hard to decorate the house and prepare refreshments. On the appointed evening, a mob of dirty, profane teenagers swarmed into the house, breaking and destroying the furnishings. During the course of the evening, Mrs Holloway said something that angered Becky. The girl struck her mother and left her lying in a pool of blood in the bathroom.

Away from home at the time, Mr Holloway returned to find his wife helpless on the floor; he located his unconcerned daughter in the garden, dancing with friends. As he described for me the details of their recent nightmare, he spoke with tears in his eyes. His wife, he said, was still in the hospital contemplating her parental failures as she recovered from her wounds.

Parents like the Holloways often fail to understand how love and discipline interact to influence the attitudes of a child. These two aspects of a relationship are not opposites working against each other. They are two dimensions of the same quality. One demands the other. Disciplinary action is not an assault on parental love; it is a function of it. Appropriate punishment is not something parents do *to* a beloved child; it is something done *for* him or her. That simple understanding when Becky was younger could have spared the Holloways an adolescent nightmare.

Their attitude when Becky rebelled as a toddler should have been, 'I love you too much to let you behave like that.' For the small child, word pictures can help convey this message more clearly. The following is a story I used with our very young children when they crossed the line of unacceptable behaviour.

> I knew of a little bird who was in his nest with his mummy. The mummy bird went off to find some worms to eat, and she told the little bird not to get out of the nest while she was gone. But the little bird didn't obey her. He jumped out of the nest and fell to the ground where a big cat got him. When I tell you to obey me, it is because I know what is best for you, just as the mummy bird did with her baby bird. When I tell you to stay in the front garden, it's because I don't want you to run into the street and get hit by a car. I love you, and I don't want anything to happen to you. If you don't obey me, I'll have to spank you to help you remember how important it is. Do you understand?

My own mother had an unusually keen understanding of good disciplinary procedures, as I have indicated. She was very tolerant of my childishness, and I found her reasonable on most issues. If I was late coming home from school and I could explain what caused the delay, that was the end of the matter. If I didn't get my work done, we could sit down and reach an agreement for future action. But there was one matter on which she was absolutely rigid: she did not tolerate insolence. She knew that answering back and what she called 'lip' were a child's most potent weapon to defiance and had to be discouraged.

I learned very early that if I was going to launch a flippant attack on her, I had better be standing at least twelve feet away. This distance was necessary to avoid an instantaneous response—usually aimed at my backside.

The day I learned the importance of staying out of reach shines like a neon light in my mind. I made the costly mistake of being cheeky to her when I was about four feet away. I knew I had crossed the line and wondered what she would do about it. It didn't take long to find out. Mum wheeled around to grab something with which to express her displeasure, and her hand landed on a girdle. Those were the days when a girdle was lined with supports and mysterious panels. She drew back and swung that abominable garment in my direction, and I can still hear it whistling through the air. The intended blow caught me across the chest, followed by a multitude of straps and buckles, wrapping themselves around my midsection. She gave me an entire thrashing with one blow! But from that day forward, I measured my words carefully when addressing my mother. I never spoke disrespectfully to her again, even when she was seventy-five years old.

I have shared that story many times through the years, to an interesting response. Most people found it funny and fully understood the innocuous meaning of that moment. A few others, who had never met my mother and had no knowledge of her great love for me, quickly condemned her for the abusiveness of that event. One Christian psychologist even wrote a chapter in his book on the viciousness of that spanking. Another man in Wichita, Kansas, was so furious with me for telling the story that he refused to come to hear me speak. Later he admitted he had misread the word 'girdle', thinking my mother had hit me with a *griddle*.

If you're inclined to agree with the critics, please hear me out. I am the only person on earth who can report accurately the impact of my mother's action. I'm the only one who lived it. And I'm here to tell you that the girdle-blow was an act of love! My mother would have laid down her life for me in a heartbeat, and I always knew it. She would not have harmed a hair on my fuzzy head. Yes, she was angry at my insolence, but her sudden reaction was a corrective manoeuvre. We both knew I richly deserved it. And that is why the momentary pain of that event did not assault my self-worth. Believe it or not, it made me feel loved. Take it or leave it, Dr Psychologist, but that's the truth.

Now let me say the obvious. I can easily see how the same setting could have represented profound rejection and hostility of the first order. If I had not known I was loved . . . if I had not deserved the punishment . . . if I had been frequently and unjustly struck for minor offences . . . I would have suffered serious damage from the same whirring girdle. The minor pain was not the critical variable. The *meaning* of the event is what mattered.

This single episode illustrates why it is so difficult to conduct definitive research on child-rearing practices. The critical factors are too subjective to be randomised and analysed. That complexity also explains why social workers seeking to rescue children from abusive homes often have such problems being fair. Many good parents in loving homes have lost custody of their sons and daughters because of evidence that is misinterpreted. For example, a tiny bruise on the buttocks of a fair-skinned child may or may not indicate an abusive situation. It all depends. In an otherwise secure and loving home, that bruise may have had no greater psychological impact than a skinned knee or a stubbed toe. Again, the significant issue is not the small abrasion; it is the *meaning* behind it—the way it occurred and the overall tone of the relationship. Nevertheless, grief-stricken parents have lost their children on the basis of a single piece of evidence of that nature. We call it parent abuse.

Please don't write and accuse me of defending parents who routinely bruise and harm their children even in a minor way. It is wrong. It should not happen. But someone should have the courage to say we must look at the *total* relationship before removing a child from the security of a good home and not base a life-changing decision on a single bit of evidence.

Getting back to our theme of respect, let me emphasise that it will not work properly as a unilateral affair; it must run both ways. Parents cannot require their children to treat them with dignity if they will not do the same in return. Parents should be gentle with their child's ego, never belittling or embarrassing him or her in front of friends. Discipline should usually be administered away from the curious eyes of gloating onlookers. Children should not be laughed at if it makes them uncomfortable. Their strong feelings and requests, even if foolish, should be given an honest appraisal. They should feel that their parents 'really *do* care about me'. Self-esteem is the most fragile attribute in human nature. It can be damaged by very minor incidents, and its reconstruction is often difficult to engineer.

Thus, a father who is sarcastic and biting in his criticism of children cannot expect to receive genuine respect in return. His offspring might *fear* him enough to conceal their contempt. But revenge will often be sought in adolescence. Children know the wisdom of the old axiom, 'Don't mock the alligator until you are across the stream.' Thus, a vicious, scathing father may intimidate his household for a time, but if he does not demonstrate respect for its inhabitants, they may return his hostility when they reach the safety of early adulthood.

Full-blown toddlerhood

Before leaving the topic of respect, let's say a few words about that marvellous time of life known as toddlerhood. It begins with a bang (like the crash of a lamp or a porcelain vase) at about eighteen months of age and runs hot and heavy until about the third birthday. A toddler is the most hard-nosed opponent of law and order, and he honestly believes the universe circles around him. In his cute little way, he is curious and charming and funny and lovable and exciting . . . and selfish and demanding, and rebellious and destructive. Comedian Bill Cosby must have had some personal losses at the hands of toddlers, for he is quoted as saying, 'Give me 200 active two-year-olds and I could conquer the world.'

Children between fifteen and thirty-six months of age do not want to be restricted or inhibited in any manner, nor are they inclined to conceal their viewpoint. They resent every nap imposed on them, and bedtime becomes an exhausting, dreaded ordeal each night. They want to play with everything in reach, particularly fragile and expensive ornaments. They prefer using their pants rather than the potty, and insist on eating with their hands. And need I remind you that most of what goes in their mouths is not food? When they break loose in a shop, they run as fast as their fat little legs will carry them. They pick up the cat by its ears and then scream blue murder when scratched. They want Mummy within three feet of them all day, preferably in the role of their full-time playmate. Truly, the toddler is a tiger!

Parents who do everything right in managing these precious babies are still likely to find them hard to control. For this reason, mums and dads should not hope to make their two-year-olds act like more mature children. A controlling but patient hand will eventually succeed in settling the little anarchist, but probably not until he is between three and four. Unfortunately, however, the child's attitude towards authority can be severely damaged during his toddler years. Parents who love their cute little poppet so much that they cannot risk antagonising him may lose and never regain their control. This is the time to establish themselves, gently but persistently, as the bosses to be reckoned with.

I once dealt with a mother of a rebellious thirteen-year-old boy who snubbed every hint of parental authority. He would not come home until at least two o'clock in the morning, and deliberately disobeyed every request she made of him. Assuming that her lack of control was a long-standing difficulty, I asked if she could tell me the history of this problem. She clearly remembered when it all started: her son was less than three at the time. She carried him to his room and placed him in his cot, and he spat in her face.

She explained the importance of not spitting in

Mummy's face, but was interrupted by another moist missile. This mother had been told that all confrontations could be resolved by love, understanding and discussion. So she wiped her face and began again, at which point she was hit with another well-aimed blast. Growing increasingly frustrated, she shook him . . . but not hard enough to disrupt his aim with the next shower.

What could she do then? Her philosophy offered no honourable solution to this embarrassing challenge. Finally, she rushed from the room in utter exasperation, and her little conqueror spat on the back of the door as it shut. She lost; he won! This exasperated mother told me she never had the upper hand with her child after that night!

When parents lose these early confrontations, the later conflicts become harder to win. Parents who are too weak or tired or busy to win make a costly mistake that will haunt them during their child's adolescence. If you can't make a five-year-old pick up his toys, it is unlikely you will exercise much control during his most defiant time of life.

It is important to understand that adolescence is a condensation or composite of all the training and behaviour that has gone before. Any unsettled matter in the first twelve years is likely to fester and erupt during adolescence. The proper time to begin disarming the teenage time bomb, then, is twelve years before it arrives. As Dr Bill Slonecker, a Nashville pediatrician and very good friend, said on a *Focus on the Family* radio broadcast, 'If discipline begins on the second day of life, you're one day late.'

Dr Slonecker wasn't referring to spanking a baby or

any other physical discipline per se. Rather, he was speaking of parents being in charge—loving the child enough to establish control. All too often he saw mothers in his private practice who were afraid to lead their infants. They would call his office and frantically huff, 'My six-month-old baby is crying and seems very hot.' He would ask the women if the child had a fever, to which they would reply, 'I don't know. He won't let me take his temperature.' Those mothers had already yielded some of their authority to their infants. They would live to regret it.

I must point out that some rebellious behaviour is distinctly different in origin from the 'challenging' defiance I've been describing. A child's antagonism and stiff-lipped negativism may emanate from frustration, disappointment or rejection, and must be interpreted as a warning signal to be heeded. Perhaps the toughest task in parenthood is recognising the difference between these two distinct motives.

A child's resistant behaviour always contains a message to his parents, which they must decode before responding. That message is often phrased in the form of a question: 'Are you in charge or am I?' A distinct reply is appropriate to discourage future attempts to overthrow constituted government in the home. On the other hand, Junior's antagonism may be his way of saying, 'I feel unloved now that I'm stuck with a yelling baby brother. Mum used to care for me; now nobody wants me. I hate everybody.' When this kind of meaning underlies the rebellion, parents should move quickly to pacify its cause.

The most effective parents are those who have the skill to get behind the eyes of their child, seeing what he sees, thinking what he thinks, feeling what he feels. For example, when a two-year-old screams and cries at bedtime, one must ascertain what he is communicating. If he is genuinely frightened by the blackness of his room, the appropriate response should be quite different from if he is merely protesting about having to go to bed. The art of good parenthood revolves around the interpretation of meaning behind behaviour.

If parents intuitively *know* their child, they will be able to watch and discern what is going on in his little head. The child will *tell* them what he is thinking if they learn to listen carefully. Unless they can master this ability, however, they will continually fumble in the dark in search of a proper response.

Repeating the first point, the most vital objective of disciplining a child is to gain and maintain his respect. If the parents fail in this task, life becomes uncomfortable indeed. We'll move on now to the other four elements of a traditional approach to child rearing, discussed in the next chapter.

3

More Common Sense about Children

I indicated in the first chapter that there were certain risks associated with my being a young father and simultaneously choosing to write and speak about the discipline of children. That placed enormous pressure on our imperfect family in those days. But God gave me good children and we handled the fishbowl experience rather well. There were a few tough moments, however, that proved to be quite embarrassing.

One of those nightmares occurred on a Sunday evening in 1974, when Danae was nine and Ryan nearly five. I was asked to speak on that occasion in a church service near our home. As it turned out, I made two big mistakes that night. First, I decided to speak on the discipline of children, and second, I took my kids to the church with me. I should have known better.

After I had delivered my thought-provoking, witty, charming and informative message that evening, I stood at the front of the church to talk to parents who sought more advice. Perhaps twenty-five mothers and fathers gathered around, each asking specific questions in turn.

There I was, dispensing profound child-rearing wisdom like a vending machine, when suddenly we all heard a loud crash in the balcony. I looked up in horror to see Danae chasing Ryan over the seats, giggling and stumbling and running through the upper deck. It was one of the most embarrassing moments of my life. I could hardly go on telling the lady in front of me how to manage her children when mine were going crazy in the balcony; nor could I easily get my hands on them. I finally caught Shirley's eye and motioned for her to launch a seek-and-destroy mission on the second tier. Never again did I speak on that subject with our kids in tow.

I share that story to clarify the goal of proper child rearing. It is not to produce perfect children. Even if you implement a flawless system of discipline at home, which no one in history has done, your children will be children. At times they will be silly, destructive, lazy, selfish and—yes—disrespectful. Such is the nature of humanity. We as adults have the same problems. Furthermore, when it comes to kids, that's the way it *should* be. Boys and girls are like clocks; you have to let them run. My point is that the principles in this book are not designed to produce perfect little robots who can sit with their hands folded in the parlour thinking patriotic and noble thoughts! Even if we *could* pull that off, it wouldn't be wise to try.

The objective, as I see it, is to take the raw material with which our babies arrive on this earth, and then gradually mould it into mature, responsible and God-fearing adults. It is a twenty-year process that will bring progress, setbacks, successes and failures. When the child turns thirteen, you'll swear for a time that he's missed everything you thought you had taught . . . manners, kindness, grace and style. But then maturity begins to take over and the little green shoots from former plantings start to emerge. It is one of the richest experiences in living to watch that progression from infancy to adulthood in the span of two dynamic decades.

Let's move on now to discuss the remaining four principles in the commonsense approach to child rearing.

Communication following discipline

The best opportunity to communicate often occurs after a disciplinary event. Nothing brings a parent and child closer together than for the mother or father to win decisively after being defiantly challenged. This is particularly true if the child was 'asking for it', knowing full well he deserved what he got. The parents' demonstration of their authority builds respect like no other process, and the child will often reveal his affection after the initial tears have dried.

For this reason, parents should not dread or shrink back from confrontations with their children. These occasions should be anticipated as important events, because they provide the opportunity to convey verbal and nonverbal messages to the boy or girl that cannot be expressed at other times. Let me again stress that I am not suggesting that parents use excessive punishment in these encounters. To the contrary, a small amount of discomfort goes a long way towards softening a child's rebellious spirit. However, the spanking should be of sufficient magnitude to cause genuine tears.

After emotional ventilation, the child will often want to crumple to the breast of his parent, and he should be welcomed with open, warm, loving arms. At that moment you can talk heart to heart. You can tell him how much you love him, and how important he is to you. You can explain why he was disciplined and how he can avoid the difficulty next time. This kind of communication is often impossible with other disciplinary measures . . . such as standing the youngster in the corner or taking away his favourite toy. A resentful child usually does *not* want to talk.

A confrontation my wife once had with our daughter, Danae, can illustrate the point. Back when Danae was but a fifteen-month-old ankle-biter, Shirley wanted to build a fire in the fireplace and needed to go out behind the garage to get some wood. It was raining, so she told Danae, who was barefoot, to wait in the doorway. Having learned to talk quite early, Danae knew the meaning of the command. Nevertheless, she suddenly came skipping across the wet patio. Shirley caught her and took her back, repeating the order more sternly. But as soon as Shirley's back was turned, Danae scooted out again. It was an unmistakable act of disobedience to a clear set of instructions. Then, on a third trip, Shirley stung Danae's little legs a few times with a switch.

After her tears had subsided, the toddler came to Shirley by the fireplace and reached out her arms, saying 'Love, Mummy.' Shirley gathered Danae tenderly in her arms and rocked her for fifteen minutes. During those loving moments, she talked softly to her about the importance of obedience.

Parental warmth after such discipline is essential to demonstrate that it is the *behaviour*—not the child himself—that the parent rejects. William Glasser, the father of Reality Therapy, made this distinction very clear when he described the difference between discipline and punishment. 'Discipline' is directed at the objectional behaviour, and the child will accept its consequence without resentment. He defined 'punishment' as a response that is directed at the individual. It represents a desire of one person to hurt another; and it is an expression of hostility rather than corrective love. As such, it is often deeply resented by the child.

Although I sometimes use these terms interchangeably, I agree with Glasser's basic premise. Unquestionably, there is a wrong way to correct a child that can make him or her feel unloved, unwanted and insecure. One of the best guarantees against this happening is a loving conclusion to the disciplinary encounter.

Control without nagging

This is our third principle, and yes, it is possible! Yelling and nagging at children can become a habit, and an ineffectual one at that! Have you ever screamed at your child, 'This is the last time I'm telling you. The last time!' Parents often use anger to get action instead of using action to get action. It is exhausting and it doesn't work! Trying to control children by screaming is as utterly futile as trying to steer a car by honking the horn.

Let's consider an illustration that could represent any one of a million homes at the end of a long, intense, whirlwind day. Dead-tired, Mum feels her head pounding like a bass drum as she contemplates getting her son to have a bath and go to bed. But eight-year-old Henry does not *want* to go to bed and knows from experience that it will take his harassed mother at least thirty minutes to get him there.

Henry is sitting on the floor, playing with his games, Mum looks at her watch and says, 'Henry, it's nearly nine o'clock (a thirty-minute exaggeration), so gather up your toys and go and have your bath.' Now Henry and Mum both know that she didn't mean him to have a bath *immediately*. She merely wanted him to start *thinking* about having his bath. She would have fainted dead away if he had responded to her empty command.

Approximately ten minutes later, Mum speaks again. 'Now, Henry, it's getting later and you have school tomorrow; I want those toys picked up and then I want you in that tub!' She still does not intend Henry to obey, and he knows it. Her *real* message is, 'We're getting closer, Henry.' Henry shuffles around and stacks a box or two to demonstrate that he heard her. Then he settles down for a few more minutes of play.

Six minutes pass and Mum issues another command, this time with more passion and threat in her voice: 'Now listen, young man, I told you to get a move on, and I meant it!' To Henry, this means he must get his toys picked up and m-e-a-n-d-e-r towards the bathroom door. If his mother rapidly pursues him, then he must carry out the assignment posthaste. However, if Mum's mind wanders before she performs the last step of this ritual, or if the phone miraculously rings, Henry is free to enjoy a few minutes' reprieve.

You see, Henry and his mother are involved in a familiar one-act play. They both know the rules and the role being enacted by the opposite actor. The entire scene is preprogrammed, computerised and scripted. In actuality, it's a virtual replay of a scene that occurs night after night. Whenever Mum wants Henry to do something he dislikes, she progresses through graduated steps of phony anger, beginning with calmness and ending with a red flush and threats. Henry does not have to move until she reaches her flashpoint.

How foolish this game is. Since Mum controls Henry with empty threats, she must stay half-irritated all the time. Her relationship with her children is contaminated, and she ends each day with a pulsing migraine above her left eye. She can never count on instant obedience, because it takes her at least five minutes to work up a believable degree of anger.

How much better it is to use *action* to achieve the desired behaviour. There are hundreds of approaches that will bring a desired response, some of which involve slight pain, while others offer the child a reward. The use of rewards or 'positive reinforcement' is discussed in the next chapter, and thus will not be presented here. But minor pain or 'negative reinforcement' can also provide excellent motivation for the child.

When a parent's calm request for obedience is ignored by a child, Mum or Dad should have some means of making their youngster *want* to co-operate. For those who can think of no such device, I will suggest one: it is muscle lying snugly against the base of the neck. Anatomy books list it as the trapezius muscle, and when firmly squeezed, it sends little messengers to the brain saying, 'This hurts: avoid recurrence at all costs.' The pain is only temporary; it can cause no damage. But it is an amazingly effective and practical recourse for parents when their youngster ignores a direct command to move.

Let's return to the bedtime scene with Henry, and let me suggest how it could be replayed more effectively. To begin with, his mother should have forewarned him that he had fifteen more minutes to play. No one, child or adult, likes a sudden interruption of his activity. It would then have been wise to set the alarm clock or the stove buzzer. When the fifteen minutes passed and the buzzer sounded, Mum should have quietly told Henry to go and have his bath. If he didn't move immediately, his shoulder muscle should have been squeezed. If Henry learns that this procedure or some other unpleasantry is invariably visited upon him, he will move before the consequences ensue.

I know that some of my readers could argue that the deliberate, premeditated application of minor pain to a small child is a harsh and unloving thing to do. To others, it will seem like pure barbarism. I obviously disagree. Given a choice between a harassed, screaming, threatening mother who blows up several times a day versus a mum who has a reasonable, controlled response to disobedience, I would certainly recommend the latter. In the long run, the quieter home is better for the child, too, because of the avoidance of strife between generations.

On the other hand, when a youngster discovers there is no threat behind the millions of words he hears, he stops listening to them. The only messages he responds to are those reaching a peak of emotion, which means there is much screaming and yelling going on. The child is pulling in the opposite direction, fraying Mum's nerves and straining the parent-child relationship. But the most important limitation of those verbal reprimands is that their user often has to resort to physical punishment in the end anyway. It is also more likely to be severe, because the adult is irritated and out of control. Thus, instead of the discipline being administered in a calm and judicious manner, the parent has become unnerved and frustrated, swinging wildly at the belligerent child. There was no reason for a fight to have occurred. The situation could have ended very differently if the parental attitude had been one of confident serenity.

Speaking softly, almost pleasantly, Mum says, 'Henry, you know what happens when you don't obey me; now I don't see any reason in the world why I should have to make you uncomfortable just to get your co-operation tonight, but if you insist, I'll play the game with you. When the buzzer sounds you let me know what the decision is.'

The child then has the choice to make, and the advantages to him of obeying his mother's wishes are clear. She need not scream. She need not threaten to shorten his life. She need not become upset. She is in command. Of course, Mother will have to prove two or three times that she will apply the pain or other punishment, if necessary. Occasionally throughout the coming months, Henry will check to see if she is still at the helm. That question is easily answered.

The shoulder muscle is a surprisingly useful source of minor pain. It can be utilised in those countless situations where face-to-face confrontations occur between adult and child. One such incident happened to me back in the days when my own kids were young. I had come out of a pharmacy and there at the entrance was a stooped, elderly man, approximately seventy-five or eighty years of age. Four boys, probably aged about fourteen, had cornered him and were running circles around him. As I came through the door, one of the boys had just knocked the man's hat down over his eyes and they were laughing about how silly he looked, leaning on his cane.

I stepped in front of the elderly fellow and suggested that the boys find someone else to torment. They called me names and then sauntered off down the street. I got into my car and was gone about fifteen minutes. I returned to get something I had forgotten, and as I was getting out of my car I saw the same four boys running from a nearby hardware shop. The proprietor raced after them, shaking his fist and screaming in protest. I discovered later that they had run down the aisles in his shop, raking cans and bottles off the shelves and onto the floor. They also made fun of the fact that he was Jewish and rather overweight.

When the boys saw me coming, I'm sure they thought I viewed myself as Robin Hood II, protector of the innocent and friend of the oppressed. One of the young tormentors ran straight up to my face and stared defiantly in my eyes. He was about half my size, but obviously felt safe because he was a teenager. He said, 'You just hit me! I'll sue you for everything you're worth!'

I have rather large hands to go with my six-foot-two, thirteen-and-a-half-stone frame. It was obviously time to use them. I grasped his shoulder muscles on both sides, squeezing firmly. He immediately dropped to the ground, holding his neck. He rolled away and ran off with his friends, screaming insults back at me.

I reported the incident and later that evening received a phone call from the police. I was told the four young thugs had been harassing shopkeepers and customers along that street for weeks. Their parents refused to co-operate with the authorities, and the police felt ham-strung. Without the parents' help, they didn't know what to do. As I reflect now on that incident, I can think of no better way to breed and cultivate juvenile delinquency than for society to allow such early defiance to succeed with impunity. Leonardo da Vinci is quoted as saying, 'He who does not punish evil commands it to be done.'

Discipline outside the home is not very different from discipline inside. The principles by which children can be controlled are the same in both settings—only the appli-cation changes. A teacher, scoutmaster or youth leader who tries to control a group of children with anger is in for incredible frustration. The children will discover how far the adult will go before taking any action, and they invariably push him or her right to that line.

It is surprising to observe how often a teacher or group leader will impose disciplinary measures that children do *not* dislike. I knew a teacher, for example, who would scream and threaten and beg her class to co-operate. When they got completely out of hand, she would climb on top of her desk and blow a whistle! The kids loved it! She weighed about seventeen stone, and the children would plot during lunch and break how they could get her on top of that desk. She was inadvertently offering enter-tainment—a reward for their unruliness. It was much more fun than studying multiplication tables! Their atti-tude was much like that of Brer Rabbit, who begged the fox not to throw him in the briar patch. There was nothing they wanted more.

One should never underestimate a child's awareness that he is breaking the rules. I think most children are rather analytical about defying adult authority: they consider the deed in advance and weigh its probable consequences. If the odds are too great that justice will triumph, they'll take a safer course. This observation is verified in millions of homes where a youngster will push one parent to the limit of tolerance, but remain a sweet angel with the other. Mum whimpers, 'Rick obeys his dad perfectly, but pays no attention to me.' Rick is no dummy. He knows Mum is safer than Dad.

To summarise this point, the parent must recognise that the most successful techniques of control are those which convey something of importance to the child. Yakkity-yak discussions and empty threats carry little or no motivational power for the child. 'Why don't you pull yourself together and do what's right, Jack? What am I going to do with you, son? It seems as if I'm always having to get on at you. I just can't see why you don't do what you're told. If only for once, just once, you would act your age.' On and on goes the barrage of words.

Jack endures the endless tirades, month in, month out, year after year. Fortunately for him, he is equipped with a mechanism that allows him to hear what he *wants* to hear and screen out everything else. Just as a person living by a railway line eventually does not even hear the trains rumbling by, so Jack has learned to ignore meaningless noise in his environment. Jack (and all his contemporaries) would be much more willing to co-operate if it were clearly to his personal advantage.

Resisting materialism

Our fourth principle is this: don't saturate the child with materialism. Despite the hardships of the great depression, at least one question was easier to answer then than it is today: How can I say no to my child's materialistic desires? It was very simple for parents to tell their children that they couldn't afford to buy them everything they wanted; Dad could barely keep bread on the table. But in more opulent times, the parental task becomes less believable. It takes considerably more courage to say, 'No, I *won't* buy you Wanda Wee-Wee and Baby-Blow-Her-Nose,' than it did to say, 'I'm sorry but you know we can't afford to buy those dolls.'

A child's demand for expensive toys is carefully generated through millions of pounds spent on TV advertising by the manufacturers. The commercials are skilfully made so that the toys look like full-sized copies of their real counterparts: jet aeroplanes, robot monsters, and automatic rifles. The little consumer sits open-mouthed in utter fascination. Five minutes later he begins a campaign that will eventually cost his dad £39.95 plus batteries.

The trouble is, Dad often *can* afford to buy the new item, if not with cash, at least with his magic credit card. And when three other children in the road get the coveted toys, Mum and Dad begin to feel the pressure, and even the guilt. They feel selfish because they have indulged themselves with similar luxuries. Suppose the parents are courageous enough to resist the child's urging; he is not blocked—grandparents are notoriously easy to 'con'. Even if the youngster is unsuccessful in getting his parents or grandparents to buy what he wants, there is an annual, foolproof resource: Santa Claus! When Junior asks Santa to bring him something, his parents are in an inescapable trap. What can they say? 'Santa can't afford it'? Is the jolly fat man in the red suit really going to forget and disappoint him? No, the toy will be on Santa's sleigh.

Some would ask, 'And why not? Why shouldn't we let our children enjoy the fruits of our good times?' Certainly I would not deny boys and girls a reasonable quantity of the things they crave. But many children are inundated with excesses that work towards their detriment. It has been said that prosperity offers a greater test of character than does adversity, and I'm inclined to agree.

There are few conditions that inhibit a sense of appreciation more than for a child to feel he is entitled to whatever he wants, whenever he wants it. It is enlightening to watch as a boy or girl tears open stacks of presents at a birthday party or perhaps at Christmas time. One after another, the expensive contents are tossed aside with little more than a glance. The child's mother is made uneasy by his lack of enthusiasm and appreciation, so she says, 'Oh Marvin! Look what it is. It's a little tape recorder! What do you say to Grandmother? Give Grandmother a big hug. Did you hear me, Marvin? Go and give Granny a big hug and kiss.'

Marvin may or may not choose to make the proper noises to Grandmother. His lack of exuberance results from the fact that prizes which are won cheaply are of little value, regardless of the cost to the original purchaser.

There is another reason that the child should be denied some of the things he thinks he wants. Although it sounds paradoxical, you actually cheat him of pleasure when you give him too much. A classic example of this saturation principle is evident in my household each year during the Thanksgiving season. Our family is blessed with several of the greatest cooks who ever ruled a kitchen, and several times a year they do their 'thing'. The traditional Thanksgiving dinner consists of turkey, dressing, cranberries, mashed potatoes, sweet potatoes, peas, hot rolls, two kinds of salad, and six or eight other dishes.

Prior to my heart attack in 1990, I joined my family in a disgraceful but wonderful gastronomic ritual during the holiday season. We all ate until we were uncomfortable, not saving room for dessert. Then the apple pie, pound cake and fresh ambrosia were brought to the table. It just didn't seem possible that we could eat another bite, yet somehow we did. Finally, taut family members began to stagger away from their plates, looking for a place to fall.

Later, about three o'clock in the afternoon, the internal pressure began to subside and someone passed the sweets around. As the usual time for the evening meal arrived, no one was hungry, yet we had come to expect three meals a day. Turkey sandwiches were constructed and consumed, followed by another helping of pie. By this time, everyone was a bit bleary-eyed, absent-mindedly eating what they neither wanted nor enjoyed. This ridiculous ritual continued for two or three days, until the thought of food became rather disgusting. Whereas eating ordinarily offers one of life's greatest pleasures, it loses its thrill when the appetite for food is satisfied.

There is a broader principle to be considered here. Pleasure occurs when an intense need is satisfied. If there is no need, there is no pleasure. A simple glass of water is worth more than gold to a man dying of thirst. The analogy to children should be obvious. If you never allow a child to want something, he never enjoys the pleasure of receiving it. If you buy him a tricycle before he can walk, a bicycle before he can ride, a car before he can drive, and a diamond ring before he knows the value of money, he accepts these gifts with little pleasure and less appreciation. How unfortunate that such a child never had the chance to long for something, dreaming about it at night and plotting for it by day. He might have even got desperate enough to work for it. The same possession that brought a yawn could have been a trophy and a treasure. I suggest that you show your child the thrill of temporary deprivation; it's more fun and much less expensive.

Before leaving this thought, let me share a relevant illustration from the closing days of my father's life. He had suffered a massive heart attack, which placed his future in jeopardy. As he contemplated his own passing, he became even more fascinated with life. Everything in God's creation interested him, from science to the arts. He even developed a personal knowledge of and a friendship with the birds that gathered around his house. He named them all and had many eating out of his hand. That is what led to . . . the starling incident.

For some reason, a mother bird abandoned her four baby starlings before they were able to fend for themselves. That precipitated an intense effort in the Dobson household to save the starlings by all means possible. Admittedly, they belonged to a despised, disease-ridden species, but my father was a sucker for *anything* in real need. Thus, a rescue effort was launched. A couple of weeks later, I received the following letter from my mother, describing what had happened to their feathered little friends.

Dear Family,

If I could write like you, Jim, I'd make the last eleven days come alive as your dad and I lived them in a bird world. As you know, the four surviving starlings, Eenie, Meenie, Minie and Moe, were evicted from their 'under the shingle' nest, and we adopted them. Their feathers were down like fuzz and their bodies seemed to consist of legs, wings, and mouths. They chirped constantly to be fed, after which their cries settled into a lovely lullaby. They outgrew their first cosy nest and your dad transferred them to a larger box from which they could not escape. So the only exposure they had to the outside world was the 2′ × 3′ area above their heads. They seemed to know this opening was where the action was, so they huddled together with their heads turned upward, tweet-tweeting their little tunes. When your dad peered over the top with our dog, Benji, all four birds would open their yellow beaks—chirping—'Worms! Worms!'

As the foursome grew, they sat on a tree limb where your dad placed them. Sometimes jumping to the ground, they followed him around the yard, cuddling his shoes and not letting him get more than a few inches away. Their jerky movements made it impossible to keep pace.

From the beginning, we were unsure what we should feed them. Your dad gave them soft bread and milk—dipping it with tweezers into their wide open beaks . . . along with worms, grain, and a few drops of water from an eyedropper. However, on the ninth morning, Jimmy found Moe dead. What to do! The tenth afternoon Meenie died. The eleventh night he looked down at the two remaining birds. Even while he looked at them, Minie gave a long 'chirp', lay down, stretched out his legs, and died. That left Eenie, the strongest of the birds . . . the one with the most vitality and personality. This morning, however, his vocalisations were desperate and weaker. He only lived until noon. As Jimmy bent over the box nest, Eenie recognised his presence, reached towards him and gave one last 'cheep', and was gone.

How sad we both were—that we somehow had failed the helpless creatures who tried so hard to live and fly in the beautiful sky. Your father's love for those insignificant birds and his sadness over their loss reveal the soul of the man I married and have lived with for forty-three years. Does anyone wonder why I love this man?

Your Mother

The man who was so loved by my mother was not long for this world. He died a month later while sitting at the dinner table. His last act before falling into her arms was to express a prayer of blessing on the meal he would not live to eat.

And the starlings? The best explanation for their failure to thrive is that my dad simply overfed them. He was fooled by their constant plea for food. In an effort to satisfy their need, my father actually killed the birds he sought desperately to save.

Does the point come through? We parents too, in our great love for our children, can do irreparable harm by yielding to their pleas for more and more things. There are times when the very best reply we can offer is . . . no.

Love and discipline

Establish a balance between love and discipline. We come now to the foundational understanding on which the entire parent-child relationship rests. It is to be found in a careful balance between love and discipline. The interaction of those two variables is critical and is as close as we can get to a formula for successful parenting.

We've already looked at the first factor, disciplinary control, and what the extremes of oppression and permissiveness do to a child. The other ingredient, parental love, is equally vital. In homes where children are not adored by at least one parent (or a parent-figure), they wither like a plant without water.

It has been known for decades that an infant who is not loved, touched and caressed will often die of a strange disease initially called marasmus. They simply wither up and die before their first birthday. Evidence of this emotional need was observed in the thirteenth century, when Frederick II conducted an experiment with fifty infants. He wanted to see what language they would speak if they never had the opportunity to hear the spoken word. To carry out this dubious research project, he assigned foster mothers to bathe and suckle the children, but forbade them to fondle, pet or talk to their charges. The experiment failed dramatically because all fifty infants died. Hundreds of more recent studies indicate that the mother-child relationship during the first year of life is apparently vital to the infant's survival. An unloved child is truly the saddest phenomenon in all of nature.

While the absence of love has a predictable effect on children, it is not so well known that excessive love or 'super love' imposes its hazards, too. I believe some children are spoiled by love, or what passes for love. Some parents have invested all of their hopes, dreams, desires and ambitions in their youngsters. The natural culmination of this philosophy is overprotection of the next generation.

I dealt with one anxious parent who stated that her children were the only source of satisfaction in living.

During the long summers, she spent most of her time sitting at the front room window, watching her three girls while they played. She feared that they might get hurt or need her assistance, or they might ride their bikes in the street. Her other responsibilities to her family were sacrificed, despite her husband's vigorous complaints. She did not have time to cook or clean her house; guard duty at the window was her only function. She suffered enormous tensions over the known and unknown dangers that could threaten her beloved offspring.

Childhood illness and sudden danger are always difficult for a loving parent to tolerate, but the slightest threat produces unbearable anxiety for the overprotective mum and dad. Unfortunately, the parent is not the only one who suffers; the child is often its victim, too. He or she is not permitted to take reasonable risks—risks which are a necessary prelude to growth and development. Likewise, the materialistic problems described in the previous section are often maximised in a family where the children can be denied nothing. Prolonged emotional immaturity is another frequent consequence of overprotection.

I should mention another unfortunate circumstance, which occurs too often in our society. It is present in homes where the mother and father represent opposing extremes in control. The situation usually follows a familiar pattern: Dad is a very busy man, and he is heavily involved in his work. He is gone from early morning to night, and when he does return, he brings home a briefcase full of work. Perhaps he travels frequently. During the rare times when he is at home and not working, he is exhausted. He collapses in front of the TV set to watch a football match, and he doesn't want to be bothered.

Consequently, his approach to child management is harsh and unsympathetic. His temper flares regularly, and the children learn to stay out of his way.

By contrast, Mum is much more supportive. Her home and her children are her sources of joy; in fact, they have replaced the romantic fires which have vanished from her marriage. She worries about Dad's lack of affection and tenderness for the children. She feels that she should compensate for his sternness by leaning in the other direction. When he sends the children to bed without their supper, she slips them some milk and biscuits. Since she is the only authority on the scene when Dad is gone, the predominant tone in the home is one of unstructured permissiveness. She needs the children too much to risk trying to control them.

Thus, the two parental symbols of authority act to contradict each other, and the child is caught somewhere between them. The child respects neither parent because each has assassinated the authority of the other. It has been my observation that these self-destructing forms of authority often load a time bomb of rebellion that discharges during adolescence. The most hostile, aggressive teenagers I have known have emerged from this antithetical combination.

Again, the 'middle ground' of love and control must be sought if we are to produce healthy, responsible children.

Summary

Lest I be misunderstood, I shall emphasise my message by stating its opposite. I am not recommending that your home be harsh and oppressive. I am not suggesting that you give your children a spanking every morning with their cornflakes, or that you make your boys sit in the living room with their hands folded and their legs crossed. I am not proposing that you try to make adults out of your kids so you can impress your adult friends with your parental skill, or that you punish your children whimsically, swinging and screaming when they didn't know they were wrong. I am not suggesting that you insulate your dignity and authority by being cold and unapproachable. These parental tactics do not produce healthy, responsible children. By contrast, I am recommending a simple principle: when you are defiantly challenged, win decisively. When the child asks, 'Who's in charge?' tell him. When he mutters, 'Who loves me?' take him in your arms and surround him with affection. Treat him with respect and dignity, and expect the same from him. Then begin to enjoy the sweet benefits of competent parenthood.

4

Questions and Answers

The discipline of children has become such a controversial and emotional issue, especially in the light of today's plague of child abuse, that the likelihood of misunderstanding is great in a book of this nature. To help clarify the philosophy from which I write, I have included the following questions and answers which were drawn from actual interactions with parents. Perhaps these items will put flesh on the bones of the structure I have built.

Q *You spoke of parents having a plan—a conscious goal in their approach to parenting. Would you apply that to preschoolers? What, specifically, should we be hoping to accomplish between eighteen months and five years of age?*

A There are two messages that you want to convey to preschool children, and even those up through primary school age. They are: (1) 'I love you, little one, more than you can possibly understand. You are precious to your (father) and me, and I thank God that he let me be your (mother)', and (2) 'Because I love you so much, I must teach you to obey me. That is the only way I can take care of you and protect you from things that might hurt you.'[1] Let's read what the Bible says to us: 'Children, obey your parents in the Lord, for this is right' (Eph 6:1, NIV). This is an abbreviated answer to a very important and complex question, but perhaps it will give you a place to begin formulating your own philosophy of parenting.

Q *We hear so much about the importance of communication between a parent and child. If you suppress a child's defiant behaviour, how can he express the hostility and resentment he feels?*

A The child should be free to say *anything* to his parent, including, 'I don't like you' or 'You weren't fair to me, Mummy.' These expressions of true feeling should not be suppressed, provided they are said in a respectful manner. There is a thin line between what is acceptable and unacceptable behaviour at this point. The child's expression of strong feeling, even resentment and anger, should be encouraged if it exists. But the parent should prohibit the child from resorting to name-calling and open rebellion. 'Daddy, you hurt my feelings in front of my friend, and you were unkind to me' is an acceptable statement. 'You stupid idiot, why didn't you shut up when my friends were here?!' is obviously unacceptable. If approached rationally as depicted in the first statement, it would be wise for the father to sit down and try to understand the child's viewpoint. Dad should be big enough to apologise to the child if he feels he was wrong. If he was right, however, he should calmly explain why he reacted as he did and tell the child how he can avoid the collision next time. It is possible to communicate without sacrificing parental respect, and the child should be taught how to express his discontent properly. This will be a very useful communicative tool later in life.

Q *We have an adopted child who came to us when he was two years old. He lived in fear, however, during those first couple of years, and we feel sorry for him. That's why my husband and I cannot let ourselves punish him, even when he deserves it. We also feel we don't have the right to discipline him, since we are not his biological parents. Are we doing right?*

A I'm afraid you are making a mistake commonly committed by the parents of older adopted children. They pity their youngsters too much to confront them. They feel that life has already been too hard on the little ones and believe they must not make things worse by disciplining them. As you indicated, there is often the feeling that they do not have the right to make demands on their adopted children.

These guilt-laden attitudes can lead to unfortunate consequences. Transplanted children have the same needs for guidance and discipline as those remaining with their biological parents. One of the surest ways to make a child feel insecure is to treat him as though he is different, unusual or brittle. If the parents view him as an unfortunate waif to be shielded, he will see himself that way, too.

Parents of sick and deformed children are also likely to find discipline harder to implement. A child with a withered arm or some non-fatal illness can become a little terror, simply because the usual behavioural boundaries are not established by the parents. It must be remembered that the need to be led and governed is almost universal in childhood. This need is not eliminated by other problems and difficulties in life. In some cases, the desire for boundaries is maximised by other troubles, for it is through loving control that parents express personal worth to a child.

Let me make one further comment about adopted children that should be noted. I would have answered the question differently if the adopted child had been physically abused. In cases where beatings and/or other harm occurred before the permanent home was found, it would be unwise to use corporal punishment. The memory of the early horror would probably make it difficult for a child to understand the corrective nature of the punishment. Other forms of discipline and great expressions of love are then in order for an abused child.

Q *Do you think a child should be required to say 'thank you' and 'please' around the house?*

A I certainly do. Requiring those phrases is one method of reminding the child that this is not a 'gimme-gimme' world. Even though parents cook for their children, buy for them, and give to them, the youngsters must assume a few attitudinal responsibilities in return. As I have already indicated, appreciation must be taught, and this instructional process begins with fundamental politeness.

Q *My husband and I are divorced, so I have to handle all the discipline of the children myself. How does this change the recommendations you've made?*

A Not at all. The principles of good discipline remain the same, regardless of the family setting. The procedures do become more difficult for one parent, like yourself, to implement, since you have no one to support you when the children become defiant. You have to play the role of the father *and* mother, which is not easily done. Nevertheless, children do not make allowances for your handicap. You must earn their respect, or you will not receive it.

Q *You have discussed the need for establishing boundaries within the home. Do children really want limits set on their behaviour?*

A Most certainly! After working with and around children all these years, I could not be more convinced of this fact. They derive security from knowing where the boundaries are and who's available to enforce them. Perhaps an illustration will make this more clear. There is a bridge which spans the Royal Gorge in Colorado. The bridge is suspended hundreds of feet above the canyon floor. Imagine yourself driving a car over this bridge. As a first-time traveller you are uneasy as you cross. (I knew one little fellow who was so awed by the view from the bridge that he said, 'Wow, Daddy. If you fell off here it'd kill you constantly!') Now suppose there were no guardrails on the side of the bridge; where would you steer the car? Right down the middle of the road!

Even though you wouldn't plan to hit the protective rails along the side, you'd feel more secure just knowing they were there.

The analogy to children has been demonstrated empirically. During the early days of the progressive education movement, one enthusiastic theorist removed the chain-link fence surrounding the nursery school playground. He thought children would feel more freedom of movement without the visible barrier surrounding them. When the fence was removed, however, the boys and girls huddled near the centre of the playground. Not only did they not wander away, they didn't even venture to the edge of the grounds.

There is security in defined limits. When the home atmosphere is as it should be, children live in utter safety. They never get into trouble unless they deliberately ask for it, and as long as they stay within the limits, there is happiness and freedom and acceptance. If this is what is meant by 'democracy' in the home, then I favour it. If it means the absence of boundaries, or that children set their own boundaries in defiance of parents, then I'm unalterably opposed to it.

Q *Permissiveness is a relative term. Please describe its meaning to you.*

A When I use the term permissiveness, I refer to the absence of effective parental authority, resulting in the lack of boundaries for the child. This word represents tolerance of childish disrespect, defiance, and the general confusion that occurs in the absence of adult leadership.

Q *I have never spanked my three-year-old because I am afraid it will teach her to hit others and be a violent person. Do you think I am wrong?*

A You have asked a vitally important question that reflects a common misunderstanding about child management. First, let me emphasise that it *is* possible . . . even easy . . . to create a violent and aggressive child who has observed this behaviour at home. If he is routinely beaten by hostile, volatile parents, or if he witnesses physical violence between angry adults, or if he feels unloved and unappreciated within his family, the child will not fail to notice how the game is played. Thus, corporal punishment that is not administered according to very carefully thought-out guidelines is a dangerous thing. Being a parent carries *no* right to slap and intimidate a child because you have had a bad day or are in a lousy mood. It is this kind of unjust discipline that causes some well-meaning authorities to reject corporal punishment altogether.

Just because a technique is used wrongly, however, is no reason to reject it altogether. Many children desperately need this resolution to their disobedience. In those situations when the child fully understands what he is being asked to do or not to do but refuses to yield to adult leadership, an appropriate spanking is the shortest and most effective route to an attitude adjustment. When he lowers his head, clenches his fists, and makes it clear he is going for broke, justice must speak swiftly and eloquently. Not only does this response not create aggression in a boy or girl, it helps them control their impulses and live in harmony with various forms of benevolent authority throughout life. Why? Because it is in harmony with nature itself. Consider the purpose of minor pain in a child's life.

Suppose two-year-old Peter pulls on a tablecloth and a vase of roses which was on it tips over the edge of the table, cracking him between the eyes. From this pain, he learns that it is dangerous to pull on the tablecloth unless he knows what sits on it. When he touches a hot stove, he quickly learns that heat must be respected. If he lives to be 100, he will never again reach out and touch the red-hot coils of a stove. The same lesson is learned when he pulls the doggy's tail and promptly receives a neat row of teeth marks across the back of his hand, or when he climbs out of his high chair when Mum isn't looking and discovers all about gravity.

For three or four years, he accumulates bumps, bruises, scratches and burns, each one teaching him about life's boundaries. Do these experiences make him a violent person? No! The pain associated with these events teaches him to avoid making the same mistakes again. God created this mechanism as a valuable vehicle for instruction.

Now when a parent administers a reasonable spanking in response to wilful disobedience, a similar non-verbal message is being given to the child. He must understand that there are not only dangers in the physical world to be avoided. He should also be wary of dangers in his social world, such as defiance, insolence, selfishness, temper tantrums, behaviour that puts his life in danger, and so on. The minor pain that is associated with this deliberate misbehaviour tends to inhibit it, just as discomfort works to shape behaviour in the physical world. Neither conveys hatred. Neither results in rejection. Neither makes the child more violent.

In fact, children who have experienced corporal punishment from loving parents do not have trouble understanding its meaning. I recall my good friends, Art and Ginger Shingler, who had four beautiful children whom I loved. One of them went through a difficult period where he was just 'asking for it'. The conflict came to a head in a restaurant, when the boy continued doing everything he could to be a brat. Finally, Art took him to the car park for an overdue spanking. A woman passerby observed the event and became irate. She chided the father for 'abusing' his son and said she intended to call the police. With that, the child stopped crying and said to his father, 'What's wrong with that woman, Dad?' *He* understood the discipline even if his rescuer did not. A boy or girl who knows love abounds at home will not resent a well-deserved spanking. One who is unloved or ignored will hate *any* form of discipline!

Q *Do you think you should spank a child for every act of disobedience or defiance?*

A No. Corporal punishment should be a rather infrequent occurrence. There is an appropriate time for a child to sit on a chair to 'think' about his misbehaviour, or he might be deprived of a privilege, or sent to his room for a 'time out', or made to work when he had planned to play. In other words, you should vary your response to misbehaviour, always hoping to stay one step ahead of the child. Your goal is to react continually in the way that benefits the child, and in accordance with his 'crime'. In this regard, there is no substitute for wisdom and tact in the parenting role.

Q *Where would you administer a spanking?*

A It should be confined to the buttocks area, where permanent damage is very unlikely. I do not believe in slapping a child on the face, or in jerking him around by the arms. A common form of injury seen in the casualty department of a children's hospital when I was there involved children with shoulder injuries. Parents had pulled tiny arms angrily and dislocated the shoulder or elbow. If you spank a child only on the 'behind' or on the upper part of the legs, I think you will be doing it right.

Q *Is there anyone who should never spank a child?*

A No one who has a history of child abuse should risk getting carried away again. No one who secretly 'enjoys' the administration of corporal punishment should be the one to implement it. No one who feels himself or herself out of control should react with *any* physical response. And grandparents probably should not spank their grandchildren *unless* the parents have given them permission to do so.

Q *Do you think corporal punishment will eventually be outlawed?*

A It is very likely. The tragedy of child abuse has made it difficult for people to understand the difference between viciousness to kids and constructive, positive forms of physical punishment. There are those in the Western world who will not rest until the government interferes with parent-child relationships with all the force of law. It has already happened in Sweden. If legislation is introduced, it will be a sad day for families. Child abuse will increase, not decrease, as frustrated parents explode after having no appropriate response to defiant behaviour.

Q *There is some controversy over whether a parent should spank with his or her hand or with some other object, such as a belt or paddle. What do you recommend?*

A I recommend a neutral object of some type. To those who disagree on this point, I'd encourage them to do what seems right to them. It is not a critical issue to me. The reason I suggest a switch or paddle is because the hand should be seen as an object of love—to hold, hug, pat and caress. If you're used to suddenly disciplining with the hand, your child may not know when he's about to be swatted and can develop a pattern of flinching when you suddenly scratch your head. This is not a problem if you take the time to get a neutral object.

My mother always used a small switch, which *could not* do any permanent damage. But it stung enough to send a very clear message. One day when I had pushed her to the limit, she actually sent me to the garden to cut my own instrument of punishment. I brought back a tiny little twig about eighteen centimetres long. She could not have generated anything more than a tickle with it. Thereafter, she never sent me on that fool's errand again.

As I conceded above, some people (particularly those who are opposed to spanking in the first place) believe that the use of a neutral object in discipline is tantamount to child abuse. I understand their concern, especially in cases when a parent believes 'might makes right' or loses his temper and harms the child. That is why adults must always maintain a balance between love and control, regardless of the method by which they administer disciplinary action.

Q *Is there an age when you begin to spank? And at what age do you stop?*

A There is no excuse for spanking babies or children younger than fifteen to eighteen months of age. Even shaking an infant can cause brain damage and death at this delicate age! But midway through the second year (eighteen months), a boy or girl becomes capable of knowing what you're telling them to do or not do. They can then very gently be held responsible for how they behave. Suppose a child is reaching for an electric socket or something that will hurt him. You say, 'No!' but he just looks at you and continues reaching towards it. You can see the smile of challenge on his face as he thinks, 'I'm going to do it anyway!' I'd encourage you to smack his fingers just enough to sting. A small amount of pain goes a long way at that age and begins to introduce children to the realities of the world and the importance of listening to what you say.

There is no magical time at the end of childhood when spanking becomes ineffective, because children vary so much emotionally and developmentally. But as a general guideline, I would suggest that *most* corporal punishment be finished before the age of six. It should taper off from there and stop when the child is between the ages of ten and twelve.

Q *If it is natural for a toddler to break all the rules, should he be disciplined for his defiance?*

A Many of the spankings and slaps given to toddlers could and should be avoided. They get into trouble most frequently because of their natural desire to touch, bite, taste, smell and break everything within their grasp. However, this 'reaching out' behaviour is not aggressive. It is a valuable means for learning and should not be discouraged. I have seen parents slap their two-year-olds throughout the day for simply investigating their world. This squelching of normal curiosity is not fair to the youngster. It seems foolish to leave an expensive trinket where it will tempt him, and then scold him for taking the bait. If little fat-fingers insists on handling the china cups on the lower shelf, it is much wiser to distract him with something else than to discipline him for his persistence. Toddlers cannot resist the offer of a new plaything. They are amazingly easy to interest in less fragile toys, and parents should keep a few alternatives available for use when needed.

When, then, should the toddler be subjected to mild discipline? When he openly defies his parents' spoken commands! If he runs the other way when called, purposely slams his milk glass on the floor, dashes into the street when being told to stop, screams and throws a tantrum at bedtime, hits his friends—these are the forms of unacceptable behaviour which should be discouraged. Even in these situations, however, all-out spankings are not often required to eliminate the behaviour. A firm rap on the fingers or a few minutes sitting on a chair will convey the same message just as convincingly. Spankings should be reserved for a child's moments of greatest antagonism, usually occurring after the third birthday.

I feel it is important to stress the point made earlier. The toddler years are critical to a child's future attitude towards authority. He should be patiently taught to obey, without being expected to behave like a more mature child.

Without watering down anything I have said earlier, I should also point out that I am a firm believer in the judicious use of grace (and humour) in parent-child relationships. In a world in which children are often pushed to grow up too fast, too soon, their spirits can dry out like prunes beneath the constant gaze of critical eyes. It is refreshing to see parents temper their inclination for harshness with a measure of 'unmerited favour'. There is always room for more loving forgiveness within our homes. Likewise, there's nothing that rejuvenates the parched, delicate spirits of children faster than when a light-hearted spirit pervades the home and regular laughter fills its rooms. Heard any good jokes lately?

Q *Sometimes my husband and I disagree on our discipline, and we will argue about what is best in front of our children. Do you think this is damaging?*

A Yes, I do. You and your husband should agree to go along with the decision of the other, at least in front of the children. The wisdom of the matter can be discussed later. When the two of you openly contradict each other, right and wrong begin to appear arbitrary to children.

Q *How do you feel about having a family council, where each member of the family has an equal vote on decisions affecting the entire family?*

A It's a good idea to let each member of the family know that the others value his viewpoint and opinion. Most important decisions should be shared within the group because that is an excellent way to build fidelity and family loyalty. However, the equal vote idea is carrying the concept too far. An eight-year-old should not have the same influence that his mother and father have in making decisions. It should be clear to everyone that the parents are the benevolent captains of the ship.

Q *My son obeys me at home, but is difficult to manage whenever I take him to a public place, like a restaurant. Then he embarrasses me in front of other people. Why is he like that? How can I change him?*

A Many parents do not like to punish or correct their children in public places where their disciplinary action is observed by critical onlookers. They'll enforce good behaviour at home, but the child is 'safe' when unfamiliar adults are around. In this situation, it is easy to see what the child has observed. He has learned that public places are a sanctuary where he can act any way he wishes. His parents are in a difficult situation because of their self-imposed restriction. The remedy for this situation is simple: when little Roger decides to disobey in public, respond exactly as you would at home, except that Roger should be removed to a place where there is privacy. Or, if he is older, you can promise to take up the matter as soon as you get home. Roger will quickly learn that the same rules apply everywhere, and that sanctuaries are not so safe after all.

Q *Should a child be disciplined for wetting the bed? How can you deal with this difficult problem?*

A Unless it occurs as an act of defiance after the child is awake, bed-wetting (enuresis) is an involuntary act for which he is not responsible. Disciplinary action under those circumstances is unforgivable and dangerous. He is humiliated by waking up wet anyway, and the older he gets, the more foolish he feels about it. The bed-wetter needs considerable reassurance and patience from parents, and they should try to conceal the problem from those who would laugh at him. Even good-natured humour within the family is painful when it is at the child's expense.

Bed-wetting has been the subject of much research, and there are several different causes in individual cases. In some children the problem is physiological, resulting from a small bladder or other physical difficulty. A pediatrician or a urologist may be consulted in the diagnosis and treatment of such cases.

For others, the problem is unquestionably emotional in origin. Any change in the psychological environment of the home may produce midnight moisture. During summer camps conducted for young children, the organisers often put plastic mattress covers on the beds of all the little visitors. The anxiety associated with being away from home apparently causes a high probability of bed-wetting during the first few nights, and it is particularly risky to be sleeping on the lower level of bunk beds! By the way, mattress covers are widely available and are a worthwhile investment for the home. They don't solve the problem, of course, but they do save in the 'mopping up' effort afterwards.

There is a third factor that I feel is the most frequent cause of enuresis, other than physical factors. During children's toddler years, they wet the bed because they simply have not mastered night-time bladder control. Some parents then begin getting their children up at night routinely to go to the potty. There the youngster is still sound asleep, being told to 'have a wee' or whatever. Thus, as the toddler grows older and the need arises to urinate at night, he often dreams he is being told to turn loose. Even when partially awakened or disturbed at night, the child can believe he is being ushered to the toilet. I would recommend that parents of older bed-wetters stop getting them up at night, even if the bed-wetting continues for a while.

There are other remedies which sometimes work, such as electronic devices that ring a bell and awaken the child when the urine completes an electrical circuit. If the problem persists, a pediatrician or child psychologist can guide you in seeking a solution. In the meantime, it is important to help the child maintain self-respect despite his embarrassing trouble. And whatever you do, conceal your displeasure if it exists.

A sense of humour may help. I received a letter from a

mother who wrote down her three-year-old son's bedtime prayer, 'Now I lay me down to sleep. I close my eyes, I wet the bed.'

Q *How long should a child be allowed to cry after being disciplined or spanked? Is there a limit?*

A Yes, I believe there should be a limit. As long as the tears represent a genuine release of emotion, they should be permitted to fall. But crying can quickly change from inner sobbing to an expression of protest aimed at punishing the enemy. Real crying usually lasts two minutes or less, but may continue for five. After that point, the child is merely complaining, and the change can be recognised in the tone and intensity of his voice. I would require him to stop the protest crying, usually by offering him a little more of whatever caused the original tears. In less antagonistic moments, the crying can easily be stopped by getting the child interested in something else.

Q *I have spanked my children for their disobedience and it didn't seem to help. Does this approach fail with some children?*

A Children are so tremendously variable that it is sometimes hard to believe they are all members of the same human family. Some boys and girls feel crushed from nothing more than a stern look, while others seem to require strong and even painful disciplinary measures to make a vivid impression. This difference usually results from the degree to which a child needs adult approval and acceptance. As I said earlier, the primary parental task is to get behind the eyes of the child, thereby tailoring the discipline to his unique perception.

In a direct answer to the question, it is generally not this individual variation that causes spanking to be ineffectual. When disciplinary measures fail, it is usually because of fundamental errors in their application. It is possible for twice the amount of punishment to yield half the results. I have made a study of situations where parents have told me their child ignores spankings and violates the same rule. There are five basic reasons for the lack of success.

1. *The most recurring problem results from infrequent, whimsical discipline.* Half the time the child is not disciplined for a particular act of defiance; the other half he is. Children need to know the certainty of justice. If there is a *chance* of beating the system, some will repeatedly try it.

2. *The child may be more strong-willed than the parent, and they both know it.* If he can outlast a temporary conflict, he has won a major battle, eliminating discipline as a tool in the parent's repertoire. The strongest of youngsters are tough enough to comprehend, intuitively, that the spanking *must not* be allowed to succeed. Thus, they stiffen their necks and battle it out. The solution is to outlast him and win, even if it takes a few rounds. The experience will be painful for both participants, but the benefits will come tomorrow and the next day and the day after.

3. *The parent suddenly employs a form of discipline after doing nothing for a year or two prior to that time.* It takes a child a while to respond to a new procedure, and parents might get discouraged during the adjustment

period. But take heart in knowing that discipline will be effective over time if consistently applied.

4. *The spanking may be too gentle.* If it doesn't hurt, it isn't worth avoiding next time. A slap with the hand on the bottom of a multi-nappied thirty-month-old is not a deterrent to anything. While being careful not to go too far, you should ensure he feels the message.

5. *For a few children, this technique is simply not appropriate.* The neurologically handicapped child who is hyperactive, for example, may be made more wild and unmanageable by corporal punishment. The child who has been abused may identify loving discipline with the hatred of the past. And, the very sensitive child might need a different approach. Once more, there is no substitute for knowledge and understanding of a particular boy or girl.

Q *Should teenage children be spanked for disobedience or rudeness?*

A No! Teenagers desperately want to be thought of as adults, and they deeply resent being treated like children. Spanking is the ultimate insult at that age, and they are justified in hating it. Besides, it doesn't work. Discipline for adolescents and teenagers should involve lost privileges, financial deprivation, and related forms of nonphysical retribution. Be creative!

My mother, I might note, was a master at trench warfare during my own stubborn adolescent years. My father was a full-time minister and frequently on the road, so Mum had the primary responsibility for bringing me up. I was giving my teachers a hard time during this era, and on several occasions was sent to the head's office, where I received stern lectures and a few swats with an infamous rubber hose (which was permissible back then). This discipline did not change my bad attitude, however, and my mother became increasingly frustrated with my irresponsibility and the falling standard of my schoolwork. It wasn't long before she reached her limit.

One day after school she sat me down and said firmly, 'I know you have been fooling around in school and ignoring your assignments. I also know you've been getting into trouble with your teachers.' (She always seemed to have a team of detectives who told her every detail of my private life, although today I think it was little more than a keen mind, good eyes and an unbelievable intuitive skill.) She continued, 'Well, I've thought it over, and I've decided that I'm not going to do anything about what is going on. I'm not going to punish you. I'm not going to take away privileges. I'm not even going to talk about it any more.'

I was about to smile in relief when she said, 'I do want you to understand one thing, however. If the head ever calls *me* about your behaviour, I promise you that the next day I'm going to school with you. I'm going to walk two feet behind you all day. I will hold your hand in front of all your friends in the hall and at lunch, and I'm going to enter into all your conversations throughout the whole day. When you sit in your seat, I'm going to pull my chair alongside you, or I'll even climb into the seat with you. For one full day, I will not be away from your side.'

That promise absolutely terrified me. It would have been social suicide to have my 'mummy' following me around in front of my friends. No punishment would have been worse! I'm sure my teachers wondered why there was such a sudden improvement in my behaviour and a remarkable jump in my grades near the end of my first year in secondary school. I simply couldn't run the risk of Mum getting that fatal phone call.

My mother knew that the threat of spanking is not the best source of motivation to a teenager. She had a better idea.

Q *My four-year-old frequently comes running home in tears because she has been hit by one of her little friends. I have taught her that it is not right to hit others, but now they are making life miserable for my little girl. What should I do?*

A I think you were wise to teach your daughter not to hit and hurt others, but self-defence is another matter. Children can be unmerciful to a defenceless child. When youngsters play together, they each want to have the best toys and determine the ground rules to their own advantage. If they find they can predominate by simply flinging a well-aimed fist at the nose of their playmate, someone is likely to get hurt. I'm sure there are those who disagree with me on this issue, but I believe you should teach your child to fight back when attacked.

I recently consulted with a mother who was worried about her small daughter's inability to defend herself. There was one child in their neighbourhood who would hit three-year-old Ann in the face at the slightest provocation. This little bully, named Joan, was very small and feminine, but she never felt the sting of retaliation because Ann had been taught not to fight. I recommended that

Ann's mother tell her to hit Joan back if she was hit first. Several days later the mother heard a loud altercation outside, followed by a brief scuffle. Then Joan began crying and went home. Ann walked casually into the house with her hands in her pockets, and explained, 'Joan socked me so I had to help her remember not to hit me again.' Ann had efficiently returned an eye for an eye and a tooth for a tooth. She and Joan have played together much more peacefully since that time.

Generally speaking, a parent should emphasise the stupidity of fighting. But to force a child to stand passively while being clobbered is to leave him at the mercy of his cold-blooded peers.

Q *Look over your twenty-five years of dealing with parents and children. What is the very best disciplinary advice you can offer? What technique or method will help us manage our kids better than any other you've seen attempted?*

A My answer may not be what you expected, but it represents something I've observed frequently and know to be valid. The *best* way to get children to do what you want is to spend time with them before disciplinary problems occur—having fun together and enjoying mutual laughter and joy. When those moments of love and closeness happen, kids are not as tempted to challenge and test the limits. Many confrontations can be avoided by building friendships with kids and thereby making them *want* to co-operate at home. It certainly beats anger as a motivator of little ones!

Q *I see now that I've been doing things wrong with my children. Can I undo the harm?*

A Once the child reaches adolescence, it is very late to be reversing the trends; before that time, though, you may yet be able to instil the proper attitudes in your child. Fortunately we are permitted to make a few mistakes with our children. No one can expect to do everything right, and it is not the few errors that destroy a child. It is the consistent influence of conditions throughout childhood.

5

The Miracle Tools

PART 1: REWARDING GOOD BEHAVIOUR

In the preceding chapters, we dealt with the proper parental response to a child's defiant 'challenging behaviour'. Now we turn our attention to the leadership of children where antagonism is not involved. There are countless situations where the parent wishes to increase the child's level of responsibility, but that task is not easy. How can a mother get her child to brush his teeth regularly, or pick up his clothes, or display table manners? How can she teach him to be more responsible with money? What can the parent do to eliminate obnoxious habits, such as whining, sloppiness, or apparent laziness? Is there a solution to perpetual tardiness?

These kinds of behaviour do not involve direct confrontations between parent and child, and should not be handled in the same decisive manner described previously. It would be unwise and unfair to punish a youngster for his understandable immaturity and childishness. A much more effective technique is available to use by the knowledgeable parent.

The first educational psychologist, E. L. Thorndike,

developed an understanding of behaviour in the 1920s that can be very useful for parents. He called it the 'law of reinforcement'. Later the concept became the basis for a branch of psychology known as behaviourism, which I resoundingly reject. Behaviourism was described by B. F. Skinner and J. B. Watson (mentioned earlier) and includes the unbelievable notion that the mind does not exist. One of my college textbooks referred to behaviourism as 'psychology out of its mind'. Well said! It perceives the human brain as a simple switchboard, connecting stimuli coming in with responses going out.

Despite my disagreement with the extrapolation of Thorndike's writings, there is no question that the original concept can be helpful to parents. Stated simply, the law of reinforcement reads, 'Behaviour which achieves desirable consequences will recur.' In other words, if an individual likes what happens as a result of his behaviour, he will be inclined to repeat that act. If Sally get favourable attention from the boys on the day she wears a new dress, she will want to wear the dress again and again. If Peter wins with one tennis racket and loses with another, he will prefer the racket with which he has found success. This principle is disarmingly simple, but it has interesting implications for human learning.

In the first edition of this book, I described the use of these techniques with our little dachshund, Sigmund Freud (Siggy). Old Siggy lived for fifteen years, but has now gone on to wherever roguish dogs go when they die. It was fun training this stubborn animal by the use of reinforcement, which was the *only* thing that got his attention. Most dachshunds will sit up without being taught to do so, for example, because it is a natural response for the long-bodied animals to make. But not Siggy! He was unquestionably the world's most independent animal. During the first year of his life, I thought he was a little bit 'slow' between the ears; the second year I began to think he might have been mentally deranged; eventually I came to see him as a recalcitrant, stubborn rascal who just wanted to do things his own way.

In short, it was difficult to entice Siggy to co-operate in any self-improvement programmes without offering him an edible incentive. He was particularly fond of biscuits, however, and I utilised this passion to good advantage. I propped him in a vertical position where he remained for only a second or two before falling. Then I gave him a piece of an old-fashioned, chocolate chip cookie. He loved it. I sat him up again, and I fed him the treat as he was falling. Siggy bounced all around the room, trying to take the remaining cookies away from me—but there was only one way to continue the treat. Even Siggy began to get that idea.

In about thirty minutes of this ridiculous exercise, the dachshund received the message loud and clear. Once it hit him, he rarely had four feet on the ground at one time! Throughout the day, he could be found propped up on his haunches, asking for a bit of something—anything. Eventually, I was sorry I had started the game, because I felt guilty ignoring him. After all, it was my idea in the first place, and I was compelled to find him something to eat in the kitchen.

This reinforcement technique was also useful in teaching Siggy to go and chase a ball (a fantastic demonstration of animal intelligence). I threw the ball about ten feet out in front of us, then dragged Sig by the nape of the neck to where it lay. I opened his mouth, put the ball in place, and dragged him back to the starting place. An oatmeal cookie was waiting at the finish line. It was even easier to get his co-operation this time because he began to grasp the concept of working for a reward. That idea became firmly ingrained and Siggy became rather creative in applying it to his advantage. If the family happened to eat dinner from trays in order to watch the evening news on television, Siggy stationed himself in the exact spot where everyone's line of vision crossed on the way to the tube. There he sat, bobbing and weaving and begging for a bite.

More serious attempts have been made to teach sophisticated behaviour to animals by the principles of reinforcement. The results have been remarkable. A pigeon was taught to examine radio parts moving by on a conveyor belt. The bird evaluated each component and knocked the defective ones off the track, for which he received a pellet of grain. He sat there all day long, concentrating on his work. As one might imagine, the trade unions took a dim view of this process; the pigeon did not demand coffee breaks or other fringe benefits, and his wages were disgracefully low. Other animals have been taught to perform virtually human feats by the careful application of rewards.

Let me hasten to acknowledge what some of my readers might be thinking at this point. There is an unbridgeable chasm between children and animals. What do these techniques have to do with kids? Just this: human beings are also motivated by what pleases them, and that fact can be useful in teaching responsible behaviour to boys and girls. However, it is not sufficient to dole out gifts and prizes in an unplanned manner. There are specific principles which must be followed if the law of reinforcement is to achieve its full potential. Let's consider the elements of this technique in detailed application to children.

1. Rewards must be granted quickly

If the maximum effectiveness is to be obtained from a reward, it should be offered shortly after the desirable behaviour has occurred. Parents often make the mistake of offering long-range rewards to children, but their successes are few. It is usually unfruitful to offer nine-year-old Joey a car when he is seventeen if he'll work hard at school during the next eight years. Seven- and eight-year-old children are often promised a trip to grandma's house next summer in exchange for good behaviour throughout the year. Their obedience is typically unaffected by this lure. It is unsatisfactory to offer Mary a new doll for Christmas if she'll keep her room straight in July. Most children have neither the mental capacity nor the maturity to hold a long-range goal in mind day after day. Time moves slowly for them; consequently, the reinforcement seems impossible to reach and uninteresting to contemplate.

For animals, a reward should be offered approximately two seconds after the behaviour has occurred. A mouse will learn the turns in a maze much faster if the cheese is waiting at the end than he will when a five-second delay is imposed. Although children can tolerate longer delays than animals, the power of a reward is weakened with time.

Immediate reinforcement has been utilised successfully

in the treatment of childhood autism, a major disorder which resembles childhood schizophrenia. The autistic child does not relate properly to his parents or any other people; he has no spoken language; he usually displays bizarre, uncontrollable behaviour. What causes this distressing disorder? The evidence seems to point towards the existence of a biochemical malfunction in the autistic child's neural apparatus. For whatever cause, autism is extremely resistant to treatment.

How can a therapist help a child who can neither talk nor relate to him? All prior forms of treatment have been discouragingly ineffective, which led Dr Ivar Lovaas and his colleagues to experiment many years ago with the use of rewards. At the University of California at Los Angeles, autistic children were placed on a programme designed to encourage speech. At first, a small sweet was placed into the child's mouth whenever he uttered a sound of any kind; his grunts, groans and growls were rewarded similarly. The next step was to reward him for more specific vowel sounds. When an 'o' sound was to be taught, a sweet was 'paid' for all accidental noises in the proper direction. As the child progressed, he was finally required to pronounce the names of certain objects or people to achieve the reinforcement. Two-word phrases were then sought, followed by more complicated sentence structure. Some language was taught to these unfortunate children by this simple procedure.

The same technique has been employed simultaneously in teaching the autistic child to respond to the people around him. He was placed in a small dark box which had one sliding wooden window. The therapist sat on the outside of the box, facing the child who peered out of the window. As long as the child looked at the therapist, the window remained open. However, when his mind wandered and he began gazing around, the panel fell, leaving him in the dark for a few seconds. Although no child with severe autism has been successfully transformed into a normal individual, the use of reinforcement therapy did bring some of these patients to a state of civilised behaviour. The key to this success has been the immediate application of a pleasant consequence to desired behaviour.

An understanding of how reinforcement works is not only useful in hospitals for autistic children. It also helps explain the way behaviour works at home, as we have seen. For example, parents often complain about the irresponsibility of their youngsters, yet they fail to realise that some of this lack of industriousness has been learned. Most human behaviour is learned—both the desirable and the undesirable responses. Children learn to laugh, play, run and jump; they also learn to whine, bully, pout, fight, throw temper tantrums, or be tomboys. The unseen teacher is reinforcement. The child repeats the behaviour which he considers to be successful. A youngster may be co-operative and helpful because he enjoys the effect that behaviour has on his parents; another will sulk and pout for the same reason. When parents recognise characteristics which they dislike in their children, they should set about teaching more admirable traits by allowing good behaviour to succeed and bad behaviour to fail.

Described below are the steps of a programme devised by Dr Malcolm Williamson and myself when we were both serving on the staff at the children's hospital of Los

Angeles. The system is useful with boys and girls between four and eight years of age; it can be modified in accordance with the age and maturity of the youngster.

(a) The chart on page 92 lists some responsibilities and behaviours which the parent may wish to instil. These fourteen items constitute a much greater degree of co-operation and effort than most five-year-old children can display on a daily basis, but the proper use of rewards can make it seem more like fun than work. Immediate reinforcement is the key; each evening, coloured (preferably red) dots or stars should be placed by the behaviours that were done satisfactorily. If dots are not available, the squares can be coloured with a felt-tip pen; however, the child should be allowed to chalk up his own successes.

(b) Two pennies should be granted for every behaviour done properly in a given day; if more than three items are missed in one day, no pennies should be given.

(c) Since a child can earn a maximum of twenty-eight pence a day, the parent has an excellent opportunity to teach him how to manage his money. It is suggested that he be allowed to spend only sixty to eighty pence per week of these earnings. Special trips to the shops can be planned. The daily ice cream van used to provide a handy source of reinforcement, although an increasing number of parents today are trying to limit the fat and sugar their children eat. Of the remaining £1.16 to £1.36 (maximum), the child can be required to give twenty pence in the church offering or to some other charitable recipient; he should then save about thirty pence per week. The balance can be accumulated for a long-range expenditure for something he wants or needs.

(d) The list of behaviours to be rewarded does not remain static. Once the child has got into the habit of hanging up his clothes, or feeding the puppy, or brushing his teeth, the parent should then substitute new responsibilities. A new chart should be made each month, and Junior can make suggestions for his revised chart.

This system provides several side benefits in addition to the main objective of teaching responsible behaviour. Through its use, for example, the child learns to count. He is taught to give to worthy causes. He begins to understand the concept of saving. He learns to restrict and control his emotional impulses. And finally, he is taught the meaning of money and how to spend it wisely. The advantages to his parents are equally impressive. A father of four young children applied the technique and later told me that the noise level in his household had been reduced noticeably.

Note: This plan is described almost exactly as it appeared in the original *Dare to Discipline*. Since then, I've heard many success stories and a few complaints. The most common negative comments have come from parents who said the task of keeping track of such a complex accounting system is burdensome every night. It takes fifteen or twenty minutes to put up the stars and measure out the pennies. If that is a concern in your family I would suggest that fewer goals be charted. Selecting even five important behaviours and rewarding them with three to five pence each would do the job just as well. *Make the*

My Jobs

November	14	15	16	17	18	19	20	21	22	23	24	25	26	27	28	29	30
1. I brushed my teeth without being told																	
2. I tidied my room before bedtime																	
3. I picked up my clothes without being told																	
4. I fed the fish without being told																	
5. I emptied the rubbish without being told																	
6. I obeyed Mummy today																	
7. I obeyed Daddy today																	
8. I said my prayers tonight																	
9. I was kind to little brother Billy today																	
10. I took my vitamin pill																	
11. I said 'thank you' and 'please' today																	
12. I went to bed last night without complaining																	
13. I gave clean water to the dog today																	
14. I washed my hands and came to the table when called																	
TOTAL:																	

system work for you, modifying the concept as needed. I assure you, however, it *will* work if properly applied.

If this kind of reinforcement is so successful, why has it not been used more widely? Unfortunately, many adults are reluctant to utilise rewards because they view them as a source of bribery. One of our most successful teaching devices is ignored because of a philosophical misunderstanding. Our entire society is established on a system of reinforcement, yet we don't want to apply it where it is needed most: with young children. As adults, we go to work each day and receive our pay at the end of the month. Is that bribery by the employer? Medals are given to brave soldiers; plaques are awarded to successful businessmen; watches are presented to retiring employees. Rewards make responsible effort worthwhile. That's the way the adult world works.

The main reason for the overwhelming success of capitalism is that hard work and personal discipline are rewarded in many ways. The great weakness of socialism is the absence of reinforcement; why should a man struggle to achieve if there is nothing special to be gained? This is, I believe, the primary reason communism failed miserably in the former Soviet Union and Eastern Europe. There was no incentive for creativity and 'sweat equity'.

I heard of a college chemistry course where the hardest working student in the class, Brains McGuffey, spent many long hours preparing for the first examination. The day of the test, he scored 90 points and earned a solid A. Another student, Ralph Ripoff, rarely ever opened a book. He took the big exam without any preparation and earned a whopping 50 points for his effort. An F was recorded in the grade book.

However, the lecturer was a staunch believer in social-istic principles. He was disturbed that Brains had 20 points more than he really needed to pass, and Ralph was 20 points short. This didn't seem fair to the good doctor. Thus the points were redistributed and both students passed with a gentleman's 'C'. But . . . Brains never studied for another chemistry exam. Do you blame him?

Communism and socialism are *destroyers* of motiva-tion, because they penalise creativity and effort. They reward mediocrity and slovenliness. The law of reinforce-ment is violated by the very nature of those economic systems. Free enterprise works hand in hand with human nature.

Some parents implement a miniature system of social-ism at home. Their children's wants and desires are pro-vided by the 'state', and are not linked to diligence or discipline in any way. However, they expect little John and René to carry responsibility simply because it is noble for them to do so. They want them to learn and sweat for the sheer joy of personal accomplishment. Most are not going to buy it.

Consider the alternative approach to the 'bribery' I've recommended. How are you going to get your five-year-old to perform the behaviours listed on the chart? The most frequently used substitutes are nagging, complain-ing, begging, screaming, threatening and punishing. The mother who objects to the use of rewards may also go to bed each evening with a headache, vowing to have no more children. She doesn't like to accentuate materialism in this manner, yet later she may *give* money to her child. Since her youngster never handles his own cash, he doesn't learn how to save it or spend it wisely. The toys she buys him are purchased with her money, and he values them less. But most important, he is not learning the self-discipline and personal responsibility that are possible through the careful reinforcement of that behaviour.

Admittedly, there are tasks that a child should do because he is a member of the family. Washing up or carrying out the rubbish may be expected and not reinforced. I agree that rewards should not be offered for every task done at home. But when you want your children to go above and beyond that base, such as cleaning out the garage, or if you want to reinforce a better attitude, there is a more efficient approach than nagging and threatening!

Still, the concept remains controversial. I watched the application of these contrasting viewpoints in two actual home situations. Darren's parents were philosophically opposed to the reinforcement that they called bribes. Consequently, he was not rewarded (paid) for his efforts around the home. Darren hated his work because there was no personal gain involved in the effort; it was something to be tolerated.

When he had to mow the lawn on Saturday, he would drag himself out to the disaster area and gaze with unfocused eyes at the depressing task before him. As might be expected, he did a miserably poor job because he was absolutely devoid of motivation. This sloppiness bought a tongue-lashing from his dad, which hardly made the experience a pleasant one. Darren's parents were not stingy with him. They supplied his needs and even gave him some spending money. When the fair came to town, they would provide money for him to spend. Because their gifts were not linked to his responsible efforts, the money provided no source of motivation. Darren grew up hating to work; his parents had inadvertently reinforced his irresponsibility.

Brian's parents took a different view. They felt that he should be paid for the tasks that went beyond his regular household duties. He was not rewarded for carrying out the rubbish or tidying his room, but he received money for painting the fence on Saturday. This hourly wage was a respectable amount, comparable to what he *could* earn outside the family. Brian loved his work. He'd get up in the morning and attack the weeds in his garden. He would count his money and work and look at his watch and work and count his money. At times he rushed home from school to get in an hour or two before dark. He opened his own bank account and was very careful about how he surrendered his hard-earned cash. Brian enjoyed great status in his neighbourhood because he always had money in his pocket. He didn't spend it very often, but he could have done so at any given moment. That was power! At one point he drew all of his money out of the bank and asked for the total amount in new five pound notes. He then carefully placed his three brand-new notes in his top drawer, and displayed them casually to Darren and his other penniless friends. Work and responsibility were the keys to this status, and he learned a good measure of both.

Brian's parents were careful never to give him a penny. They bought his clothes and necessities, but he purchased his own toys and personal indulgences. From an economic point of view, they spent no more money than did Darren's mum and dad; they merely linked each penny to the behaviour they desired. I believe their approach was the more productive of the two.

As implied before, it is very important to know when to use rewards and when to resort to punishment. It is not recommended that rewards be utilised when the child has challenged the authority of the parent. For example, Mum may say, 'Pick up your toys, Lisa, because friends are coming over,' and Lisa refuses to do so. It is a mistake for Mum then to offer a sweet if Lisa will comply with her request. She would actually be rewarding her defiance.

If there is still confusion about how to respond in this kind of direct conflict, I suggest the reader take another look at Chapters 1 to 4 of this book. Rewards should not be used as a substitute for authority; reward and punishment each has its place in child management, and reversals bring unfortunate results.

2. Rewards need not be material in nature

When my daughter was three years of age, I began to teach her some pre-reading skills, including the alphabet. In those days, I worried less about nutrition than I do now, and I often used bits of chocolate as my reinforcement. Late one afternoon I was sitting on the floor drilling Danae on several new letters when a tremendous crash shook the house. The whole family rushed outside to see what had happened and observed that a teenager had wrecked his car in our quiet residential neighbourhood. The boy was not badly hurt, but his car was upside-down in the street. We made the necessary phone call to the police, and it was not until the excitement began to lessen that we realised our daughter had not followed us out of the house.

I returned to the den, where I found her elbow-deep in the two-pound bag of chocolate sweets I had left behind. She had put at least a quarter of a pound of chocolate into her mouth, and most of the remainder was distributed around her chin, nose and forehead. When she saw me coming, she managed to jam another handful into her chipmunk cheeks. From this experience, I learned one of the limitations of using material, or at least edible, reinforcement.

Anything that is considered desirable to an individual can serve as reinforcement for his behaviour. The most obvious rewards for animals are those which satisfy physical needs, although humans are further motivated to resolve their psychological needs. Some children, for example, would rather receive a sincere word of praise than a five pound note, particularly if the adult approval is expressed in front of other children. Children and adults of all ages seek constant satisfaction of their emotional needs, including the desire for love, social acceptance and self-respect. Additionally, they hope to find excitement, intellectual stimulation, entertainment and pleasure.

Most children and adults are keenly interested in what their associates think and say. As a result, verbal reinforcement can be the strongest motivator of human behaviour. Consider the tremendous impact of the following comments:

Here comes Phil—the ugliest guy in school.

Louise is so stupid! She never knows the right answer in class.

Joe will get caught out. He always does.

These unkind words burn like acid to the children they describe, causing them to modify future behaviour. Phil may become quiet, withdrawn and easily embarrassed. Louise will probably display even less interest in her schoolwork than before, appearing lazy to her teachers. Joe may give up football and other athletic endeavours.

We adults are equally sensitive to the idle comments of our peers. It is often humorous to observe how vulnerable we are to the casual remarks of our friends (and even our enemies). 'You've gained a few pounds, haven't you, Martha?' Martha may choose to ignore the comment for the moment, but she will spend fifteen minutes in front of the mirror that evening and start a diet the next morning.

'Ralph is about your age, Pete; I'd say he is forty-six or forty-eight years old.' Pete is only thirty-nine, and the blood drains from his face; the new concern over his appearance may be instrumental in his decision to purchase a hairpiece the following month. Our hearing apparatus is more attuned to this kind of personal evaluation than any other subject, and our sense of self-respect and worthiness emerge largely from these unintentional messages.

Verbal reinforcement should permeate the entire parent-child relationship. Too often our parental instruction consists of a million 'don'ts' which are jammed down the child's throat. We should spend more time rewarding him for the behaviour we desire, even if our 'reward' is nothing more than a sincere compliment. Remembering the child's need for self-esteem and acceptance, the wise parents can satisfy those important longings while using them to teach valued concepts and behaviour. A few examples may be helpful:

Mother to daughter: 'You certainly coloured nicely within the lines of the picture, Ruth. I like to see that kind of neat artwork. I'm going to put this on the refrigerator.'

Mother to husband in son's presence: 'Neil, did you notice how Don put his bicycle in the garage tonight? He used to leave it out until we told him to put it away; he is becoming much more responsible, don't you think?'

Father to son: 'I appreciate your being quiet while I was calculating the income tax, Son. You were very thoughtful. Now that I have that job done, I'll have more time. Why don't we plan to go to the zoo next Saturday?'

Mother to small son: 'Kevin, you haven't sucked your thumb all morning. I'm very proud of you. Let's see how long you can go this afternoon.'

It is unwise for a parent to compliment the child for behaviour she does not admire. If everything the child does earns him a big hug and a pat on the back, Mum's approval gradually becomes meaningless. Specific behaviour warranting genuine compliments can be found if it is sought, even in the most mischievous youngster.

Well, let's pause for a few relevant questions and answers, and then return in the next chapter to some additional thoughts about the law of reinforcement.

Q *Can rewards be employed in a church or Sunday school?*

A I have seen reinforcement utilised with great effectiveness in a Christian Sunday school. Instead of earning money, children accumulated 'talents' which resembled toy money of various denominations. (The concept of talents was taken from Jesus' parable in Matthew 25:15.)

The children earned talents by memorising Scripture verses, being punctual on Sunday morning, having perfect attendance, bringing a friend, and so on. This system of currency was then used to obtain new items from those on display. Bibles, pens, books, puzzles and other religious or educational prizes were available for selection.

The children's work blossomed in the church where this system was employed. However, some people may oppose this materialistic programme in a church setting, and that is a matter for individual evaluation.

Q *Must I praise my child all day for every little thing he does? Isn't it possible to create a spoiled brat by telling him his every move is wonderful?*

A Yes, inflationary praise is unwise. As I mentioned in an earlier book, a child quickly catches on to your verbal game and your words then lose their meaning. It is helpful, therefore, to distinguish between the concepts of *flattery* and *praise*.

Flattery is unearned. It is what Grandma says when she comes for a visit: 'Oh, look at my beautiful little girl! You're getting prettier each day. I bet you'll have to beat the boys off with a club when you get to be a teenager!' Or, 'My, what a smart boy you are.' Flattery occurs when you heap compliments upon the child for something he does not achieve.

Praise, on the other hand, is used to reinforce positive, constructive behaviour. It should be highly specific rather than general. 'You've been a good boy . . .' is unsatisfactory. 'I like the way you kept your room clean today' is better. Parents should always watch for opportunities to offer genuine, well-deserved praise to their children, while avoiding empty flattery.[1]

Q *Should a parent try to force a child to eat?*

A No. In fact, the dinner table is one potential battlefield where a parent can easily get ambushed. You can't win there! A strong-willed child is like a good military general who constantly seeks an advantageous place to take on the enemy. He need look no further. Of all the common points of conflict between generations . . . bedtime, hair, clothes, schoolwork, etc, the advantages at the table are all in the child's favour! Three times a day, a very tiny child can simply refuse to open his mouth. No amount of coercing can make him eat what he doesn't want to eat.

I remember one three-year-old who was determined not to eat his peas, and a father who had made up his mind the squishy little vegetables were going down. It was a classic confrontation between the irresistible force and an immoveable object. Neither would yield. After an hour of haranguing, threatening, cajoling and sweating, the father had not achieved his goal. The tearful toddler sat with a forkload of peas pointed ominously at his sealed lips.

Finally, through sheer intimidation, the dad managed to get one bite of peas in place. But the lad wouldn't swallow them. I don't know everything that went on afterwards, but the mother told me they had no choice but to put the child to bed with the peas still in his mouth. They were amazed at the strength of his will.

The next morning, the mother found a little pile of mushy peas where they had been expelled at the foot of the bed! Score one for Junior, none for Dad. Tell me in what other arena a two-and-half-stone child could defeat a fourteen-stone man?

Not every toddler is this tough, of course. But *many* of them will gladly do battle over food. It is their ideal power game. Talk to any experienced parent or grandparent and they will tell you this is true. The sad thing is that these conflicts are unnecessary. Children will eat as much as they need if you keep them from indulging in the wrong stuff. They will not starve. I promise!

The way to deal with a poor eater is to set good food before him. If he claims not to be hungry, wrap the plate, put it in the refrigerator and send him cheerfully on his way. He'll be back in a few hours. God has put a funny little feeling in his tummy that says, 'Gimme food!' When this occurs, *do not* put sweets, snacks or confectionery food in front of him. Simply retrieve the earlier meal, warm it up and serve it again. If he protests, send him out to play again. Even if twelve hours or more goes by, continue this procedure until food . . . all food . . . begins to look and smell wonderful. From that time forward, the battle over the dinner table should be history.

Q *You stated earlier that you do not favour spanking teenagers. What would you do to encourage co-operation from my fourteen-year-old who deliberately makes a nuisance of himself? He throws his clothes around, refuses to help with any routine tasks in the house, and pesters his little brother to death. What am I to do about it?*

A The principles of reinforcement are particularly useful with teenagers, because such rewards appeal to youngsters during this typically self-centred time of life. However, laziness is an unavoidable fact of life with many adolescents. Their lack of industriousness and general apathy has a physiological origin. Their energy during early adolescence is being redirected into rapid growth. Also, glandular changes require a physical re-adjustment. For several years they may want to sleep until noon and drag themselves around until it comes time to do something that suits their fancy. If *any* system will succeed in charging their sluggish batteries, it will probably involve an incentive of some variety. The following three steps can be followed in implementing a system of reinforcement with a sixteen-year-old:

1. *Decide what is important to the youngster for use as an incentive.* An allowance is an easily available source of motivation. Teenagers have a great need for cold cash today. A routine date with a girl from school might cost ten pounds or more—in some cases *far* more. Another incentive may involve a fashionable article of clothing which would not ordinarily be within your teenager's budget. Offering him or her a means of obtaining such luxuries is a happy alternative to the whining, crying, begging, complaining and pestering that might occur otherwise. Mum says, 'Of course you can have the ski sweater, but you'll have to earn it.' Once an acceptable motivator is agreed upon, the second step can be implemented.

2. *Formalise the agreement.* A contract is an excellent means of settling on a common goal. Once an agreement has been written, it is signed by the parent and teenager. The contract may include a point system which enables your teenager to meet the goal in a reasonable time

period. If you can't agree on the point values, you could allow for binding arbitration from an outside party. Let's examine a sample agreement in which Marshall wants a compact disc player, but his birthday is ten months away and he's flat broke. The cost of the player is approximately £100. His father agrees to buy the device if Marshall earns 10,000 points over the next six to ten weeks doing various tasks. Many of these opportunities are outlined in advance, but the list can be lengthened as other possibilities become apparent:

Points

(a) For making bed and cleaning room each morning	50
(b) For each hour of studying	150
(c) For each hour of house or garden work done	300
(d) For being on time at breakfast and dinner	40
(e) For babysitting siblings per hour	150
(f) For washing car each week	250
(g) For getting up by 8:00 am Saturday morning	100

While the principles are almost universally effective, the method of application must be varied. With a little imagination, you can create a list of chores and point values that work in your family. It's important to note that points can be gained for co-operation and lost for resistance. Disagreeable and unreasonable behaviour can be penalised 50 points or more. (However, penalties must be imposed fairly and rarely or the entire system will crumble.) Also, bonus points can be awarded for behaviour that is particularly commendable.

    3. *Establish a method to provide immediate rewards.*

Remember that prompt reinforcement achieves the best results. This is necessary to sustain teenagers' interest as they move towards the ultimate goal. A thermometer-type chart can be constructed, with the point scale listed down the side. At the top is the 10,000-point mark, beside a picture of a compact disc player or other prize. Each evening, the daily points are totalled and the red portion of the thermometer is extended upwards. Steady, short-term progress might earn Marshall a bonus of some sort—perhaps a CD of his favourite musician or a special privilege. If he changes his mind about what he wishes to buy, the points can be diverted to another purchase. For example, 5,000 points is 50 per cent of 10,000 and would be worth £50 towards another purchase. However, do not give your child the reward if he does not earn it. That would eliminate future uses of reinforcement. Likewise, do not deny or postpone the goal once it is earned. The system described above is not in concrete. It should be adapted to the age and maturity of the adolescent. One youngster would be insulted by an approach that would thrill another.

6

The Miracle Tools

PART 2: DISCOURAGING BAD BEHAVIOUR

As we have been discussing, increasing a child's level of responsibility and self-discipline is not a simple task. It must be taught by parents with a specific game plan. But the job is made easier by utilising the law of reinforcement. In the previous chapter, we examined two specific principles which maximise the benefits of this technique. These were (1) to grant rewards immediately, and (2) utilise non-material rewards, such as praise, hugs and plain old attentiveness, along with financial and material reinforcement.

We'll turn our attention now to the remaining three principles, beginning with this:

3. Withholding rewards

Almost any behaviour that is learned through reinforcement can be eliminated if the reward is withheld long enough. It is an established fact that unreinforced behaviour will eventually disappear. This process, called *extinction* by psychologists, can be very useful to parents and teachers who want to alter the behaviour of children.

Again, the animal world provides many interesting examples of extinction. For example, the walleyed pike is a large fish with a big appetite for minnows. If placed in a tank of water with its small prey, the pike will soon be in the tank alone. However, an interesting thing occurs when a plate of glass is slipped into the tank, separating the pike from the minnows. The pike cannot see the glass and hits it solidly in pursuit of its dinner. Again and again it will swim into the glass, bumping whatever one calls the front end of a walleyed pike. Clearly, behaviour is *not* being reinforced, and, thus, is extinguished gradually.

Eventually, the pike gives up. It has learned that the minnows are not available. The glass can then be taken from the tank, allowing the minnows to swim around their mortal enemy in perfect safety. The pike will not try to eat them. It knows what it knows: they are unreachable. Amazingly, the walleyed pike will actually starve to death while its favourite food casually swims right past its mouth.

Extinction is also utilised to restrain elephants in a circus. When the elephant is young, its foot is chained to a large, immovable cement block. The animal will pull repeatedly against the barrier without success, thereby extinguishing its escape behaviour. Later, a small rope attached to a fragile stake from which a dog could break free will be sufficient to restrain the powerful pachyderm. Again, the beast knows what it knows!

Let me say it once more: children are human and unlike the animal world in most respects. But the principle of extinction is applicable to kids as well. To eliminate an undesirable behaviour in a child, one must identify and then withhold the critical reinforcement. Let's apply this concept to a common childhood problem. Why does a child whine instead of speaking in a normal voice? Because the parent has reinforced whining! When three-year-old Karen speaks in her usual voice, her mum is too busy to listen. Actually, Karen babbles all day long, so her mother tunes out most of her verbiage. But when Karen speaks in a grating, irritating, obnoxious tone, Mum turns to see what's wrong. Karen's whining brings results; her normal voice does not. And so she becomes a whiner.

To extinguish the whining, one must simply reverse the reinforcement. Mum should begin by saying, 'I can't hear you because you're whining, Karen. I have funny ears. They just can't hear whining.' After this message has been communicated for a day or two, Mum should ignore all moan-tones. On the other hand, she should offer immediate attention to a request made in a normal voice.

If this control of reinforcement is applied properly, it *will* achieve the desired results. Nearly all learning is based on this principle, and the consequences are certain and predictable. Of course, Grandma and Uncle Albert may continue to reinforce the behaviour you are trying to extinguish, and thereby keep it alive. So teamwork is a must, especially between parents.

Extinction is not only a tool for use in a deliberate training programme. It also happens accidentally at times. Consider the case of four-year-old Mark. His mother and father were concerned about his temper tantrums, especially since he habitually threw them when his parents least wanted him to misbehave. For example, when guests were visiting their home, he would explode just before bedtime. The same outbursts occurred in restaurants, church services, and other public places.

Mark's parents were no strangers to discipline, and they tried every approach on their little rebel. They spanked him, stood him in the corner, sent him to bed early, and shamed and scolded him. Nothing worked. The temper tantrums continued regularly.

Then one evening Mark's parents were both reading a newspaper in their living room. They had said something that angered their son, and he fell on the floor in a rage. He screamed and whacked his head on the carpet, kicking and flailing his small arms. They were totally exasperated at that point and didn't know what to do, so they did nothing. They continued reading the paper in stony silence, which was the last thing the little tornado expected. He got up, looked at his father, and fell down for Act Two. Again his parents made no response. By this time they were glancing at one another knowingly and watching Mark with curiosity. Again, his tantrum stopped abruptly. He approached his mother, shook her arm, then collapsed for Act Three. They continued ignoring him. His response? This child felt so silly flapping and crying on the floor that he never threw another tantrum.

Now it can be told: the illustration cited above was included in the first edition of *Dare to Discipline,* back in 1970. It is time now to reveal that Mark was not the real name of that child. It was Jim. Alas, *I* was the brat in the story. And I can tell you, it's no fun staging a performance if the crowd won't come!

It is clear that the reinforcement for my tantrums was parental manipulation. Through violent behaviour, I had got those big, powerful adults upset and distraught. I must have loved it. With most children, tantrums are a form of challenging behaviour that can be eliminated by one or more appropriate spankings. For a few like me, however, something else was going on. Like a pyromaniac, I enjoyed seeing how much commotion I could precipitate. That, in itself, was my reward.

Although my parents extinguished this negative behaviour in one episode, it usually takes much longer. It is important to understand the typical rate at which a characteristic will disappear without reinforcement.

Consider again the example of the pigeon checking radio parts, mentioned in the previous chapter. Initially, the bird missed all the defective components, and only gradually recognised a higher percentage. As illustrated in Figure A (on page 112), the pigeon eventually identified 100 per cent of the parts, and continued with perfect accuracy while the reinforcement (grain) was paid for each success.

Suppose the reinforcement was then withheld. The pigeon would continue to intercept the broken parts with perfect accuracy, but not for long. Soon he would begin to miss a few bad components. If he continued to work for nothing, he would become more and more distracted and disinterested in his task. By the end of the day, he would miss all or most of the defective parts.

However, the following day, he would again go to work as before. *Even though the behaviour is extinguished one day, it will probably return the next.* This reawakening is called 'spontaneous recovery'. Each day, the behaviour returns as illustrated in Figure B. But the accuracy is less and the daily extinction occurs more quickly than the day before.

This principle is important in extinguishing undesirable behaviour in children. A parent or teacher should

Figure A

Figure B

not become discouraged if an extinguished behaviour reappears. Its complete elimination may require considerable time.

The principle of extinction has helped many people break bad habits. One such system is designed for those who want to give up smoking. It is based on eliminating the pleasantness (reinforcement) usually produced by inhaling cigarette smoke. To do this, a tube filled with very stale, concentrated tobacco smoke is aimed at the smoker's face. Whenever the individual takes a puff from his cigarette, he is shot in the face with the putrid smoke from the tube. The smoker begins to associate cigarettes with the foul blast in his face, and by this means sometimes develops a strong dislike for smoking. Unfortunately, nicotine is one of the most addictive narcotics known, and the chemical impact is extremely difficult to overcome.

Extinction can also help children overcome some of their unnecessary fears. I once consulted with a mother who was very concerned about her three-year-old daughter's fear of the dark. Despite the use of a night light and leaving the bedroom door open, little Megan was afraid to stay in her room alone. She insisted that her mother sit with her until she went to sleep each evening, which was extremely time-consuming and inconvenient. If Megan happened to awaken in the night, she would call for help. It was apparent that she was genuinely frightened.

Fears such as these are not innate: they have been learned. If parents truly realised this, they would be more careful about what they say and how they act. The fact is, youngsters are amazingly perceptive and often adopt the behaviours and concerns they see in adults. Even good-natured teasing can produce problems for a child. If a youngster walks into a dark room and is pounced upon from behind the door, he quickly learns that the dark is not always empty!

In Megan's case, it was unclear where she learned to fear the dark, but I believe her mother inadvertently magnified the problem. In her concern for her daughter, she conveyed anxiety, and Megan began to think her own fears must be justified. 'Even Mother is worried about it,' she undoubtedly reasoned. Megan became so frightened that she could not walk through a dimly lit room without an escort. It was at this point that she was referred to me.

Since it is usually unfruitful to try to talk children out of their fears, I suggested that the mother *show* Megan there was nothing to be afraid of. That would help the child perceive her mother as being confident and unthreatened. So she bought a bag of sweets (okay, okay . . . I would use pieces of fruit today) and placed her chair just outside Megan's bedroom door. Megan was then offered a sweet if she spent a few seconds in her bedroom with the light on and door shut. This first step was not very threatening, and Megan enjoyed the game. It was repeated several times, and then she was asked to walk several feet into the darkened room while her mother, clearly visible on the landing, counted to ten. This was also easy, and Megan continued playing along for the sweets.

On subsequent trips, the door was shut a few inches more and the lights were lowered. Finally, Megan had the courage to enter the dark room and shut the door while her mother counted to three—then five—then eight. The time in the dark was gradually lengthened, and instead of producing fear it produced sweets: ultimate pleasure to a small child. She also heard her mother talking confidently and quietly, and knew she could come out whenever she wished. Through these means, courage was reinforced and fear extinguished.

Like the kind of reward you choose, the uses of extinction are limited only by the imagination and creativity of the parent or teacher. Try it in various settings. With a little practice and patience, you will see for yourself that one of the best methods of changing a behaviour is to withhold reinforcement while rewarding its replacement.

Moving ahead, the fourth principle of getting the most from the miracle tool is:

4. It works both ways

Parents and teachers are also vulnerable to reinforcement. Reinforcement is not only the mechanism by which *children* and *animals* learn new behaviour. Adults also modify their behaviour according to the positive and negative feedback they receive. Inevitably children sometimes train their parents, rather than the reverse, by reinforcing certain behaviours and extinguishing others.

For example, when Mum and Dad take their children to some exciting place, such as Disneyland, the youngsters put on their best behaviour. They may be sweet and co-operative—an unsubtle attempt to reinforce or reward their parents' action. In extreme cases, I have seen children adeptly manipulate their parents to get what they want or the behaviour they prefer.

A case in point is when Mum disciplines her eight-year-old daughter, only to hear, 'You don't love me any more.' Most children know their parents are anxious to convey their love, so they use this delicate issue to extinguish punishment. It often succeeds.

Another example is when the teacher announces, 'It is time to study health, so get out your textbooks,' and the entire class groans. For some instructors, this lack of reinforcement is difficult to tolerate, and they'll either eliminate a boring subject from their future curriculum or teach it in the most perfunctory way.

Similar phenomena occur in higher education, too. I knew of a psychology class in which the students experimented with reinforcement on their lecturer. This instructor utilised two distinct teaching methods. He either lectured from his notes, which was a dry, dismal experience for students, or he spoke extemporaneously, resulting in lively and interesting discussions. One day the students agreed before class to reward his conversational style and extinguish his formal behaviour. Whenever he used notes, they shuffled their feet, looked out of the window, yawned and whispered to each other. On the other hand, they exhibited fascination with his unstructured lessons. The lecturer responded in classic fashion. He adopted the informal approach almost exclusively, although he didn't know he was being manipulated until nearly the end of the term.

A final example is the dad who has a very low frustration tolerance with his children. He screams at them whenever they fall short of his expectations, which seems to make them obey. He has been reinforced for his screaming and becomes a loud, aggressive parent.

The point is simple: parents should be aware of their own reactions to reinforcement and make certain they are in control of the learning situation.

The fifth and final key of the law of reinforcement relates to:

5. Accidental reinforcement

Parents often reinforce undesirable behaviour and weaken behaviour they value. Perhaps the most important aspect of the past two chapters relates to accidental reinforcement. It is remarkably easy to reward undesirable behaviour in children by allowing it to succeed. Suppose, for example, that Mr and Mrs Weakknee are having dinner guests, and they put three-year-old Ricky to bed at seven o'clock. They know Ricky will cry, as he always does, but what else can they do? Indeed, Ricky cries. He begins at a low pitch and gradually builds to the decible level of a jet at takeoff.

Finally, Mrs Weakknee becomes so embarrassed by the display that she lets Ricky get up. What has the child learned? That he must cry *loudly* if he doesn't want to go to bed. Quiet protests don't work. Mr and Mrs Weakknee had better be prepared for a tearful battle the following night, too, because the response eventually succeeded. And if they forget, Ricky will undoubtedly remind them.

To explain this principle further, let's consider another scenario. An argumentative teenager, Laura Beth, never takes 'no' for an answer. She is so cantankerous that she's only homesick when she's at home. Whenever her mother is unsure whether she should allow Laura Beth to go out at night, she first tells her she *can't* go. By saying 'no' initially, Laura Beth's mum buys some extra time to think the request over. She can always change her mind, but she knows it's easier to go from 'no' to 'yes' than the other way. However, what all of this tells Laura Beth is that 'no' really means 'maybe' . . . and that 'yes' is possible if she argues and complains enough.

Many parents make the same mistake as Laura Beth's mother. They allow arguing, sulking, pouting, door slamming and bargaining to succeed. Parents should not take a definitive position on an issue until they have thought it over thoroughly and listened to the child's argument. Then they should stick tenaciously to their decision. If the teenager learns that 'no' means 'absolutely not', she is less likely to waste her effort appealing her case.

Or suppose it is Mr and Mrs Smith's tenth wedding anniversary and they are going out for dinner. As they prepare to leave, their five- and six-year-old children begin howling about being left behind. Mr Smith is vaguely familiar with the principles of reinforcement, so he offers a pack of chewing gum to the children if they'll stop crying. Unfortunately, Mr Smith has not reinforced the silence; he has rewarded the tears. The next time he and Mrs Smith leave it will be to the children's advantage to cry again. A small alternative would have changed the setting entirely. Mr Smith should have offered the chewing gum for their co-operation before the tears began to fall.

Let's apply the principle to babies and their tears. Crying is an important form of communication for infants. Through their wails we learn of their hunger, fatigue, discomfort, or nappy disaster. Although we don't want to eliminate crying in babies, it is possible to make them less noisy by minimising the reinforcement of their tears. If an infant is immediately picked up or rocked each time he cries, he may quickly observe the relationship between tears and adults' attention. How well I remember standing at the doorway of my infant daughter's nursery for several minutes, awaiting a momentary lull in the crying before going to her cot. By doing so, I reinforced the pauses rather than the howls.

Obviously, parents must be careful about the behaviours they allow to succeed. They must exercise self-discipline and patience to ensure that the tools of reinforcement and extinction are being used to encourage responsible and mature behaviour.

Q *How can I acquaint my twelve-year-old with the need for responsible behaviour throughout his life? He is desperately in need of this understanding.*

A Rather than reinvent the wheel, let me again quote from one of my other books which addresses this very issue. There, I said the overall objective during pre-adolescence is teaching the child that actions have inevitable consequences. One of the most serious casualties in a permissive society is the failure to connect those two factors: behaviour and consequences.

Too often, a three-year-old child screams insults at his mother, but Mum stands blinking her eyes in confusion. A five-year-old launches an attack on his teacher, but the school makes allowances for his age and takes no action. A ten-year-old is caught stealing CDs in a store, but is released on the plea of his parents. A fifteen-year-old steals the keys to the family car, but his father pays the fine when he is arrested. A seventeen-year-old drives his Ford Escort like a maniac and his parents pay for the repairs when he tears off the front bumper. You see, all through childhood, loving parents seem determined to intervene between behaviour and consequences, breaking the connection and preventing the valuable learning that could have occurred.

Thus, it is possible for a young man or woman to enter adulthood without knowing that life bites—that every move we make directly affects our future, and that irresponsible behaviour eventually produces sorrow and pain. Such a person applies for his first job and arrives late for work three times during the first week. Later, when fired in a flurry of hot words, he becomes bitter and frustrated. It was the first time in his life that Mum and Dad couldn't come running to rescue him from the unpleasant consequences. Unfortunately, many parents still 'bail out' their children long after they are grown and living away from home. What is the result? This overprotection produces emotional cripples who often develop lasting characteristics of dependency and a kind of perpetual adolescence.

How does one connect behaviour with consequences? By being willing to let the child experience a reasonable amount of pain or inconvenience when he behaves irresponsibly. When Barbara misses the school bus through her own dawdling, let her walk a mile or two and get to school midmorning (unless safety factors prevent this). If Janie carelessly loses her dinner money, let her skip a meal. Obviously, it is possible to carry this principle too far and become harsh and inflexible with an immature child. The best approach is to expect boys and girls to carry the responsibility that is appropriate for their age and occasionally to taste the bitter fruit that irresponsibility bears.

Q *You have referred to children who manipulate their mothers and fathers. On the other hand, isn't the parent manipulating the child by the use of rewards and punishment?*

A No more than a factory supervisor is manipulating his employees by insisting that they arrive at work at 9:00 am. No more than a policeman manipulates the speeding driver by booking him. No more than the Inland Revenue fines a taxpayer for submitting an incorrect tax return. The word 'manipulation' implies a sinister or selfish motive. I prefer the term 'leadership', which is in the best interest of everyone—even when it involves unpleasant consequences.[1]

Q *I am a teacher in a secondary school, and there are five separate classes that come to my room to be taught science each day. My biggest problem is getting those students to bring books, paper and pencils to class with them. I can lend them the equipment they need, but I never get it back. What do you suggest?*

A I faced an identical problem the year I taught in a secondary school. My students were not malicious; they just had too many other things on their minds to remember to bring their school materials. I tried various motivational techniques, but without success. I appealed to the students' desire for responsibility, but generated only yawns. I launched an emotional tirade, but that seemed like a great waste of energy for such a small issue. There had to be a better way!

I finally reached a solution based on the certainty that

young people will co-operate if it's to their advantage. I announced one morning that I no longer cared whether they brought their pencils and books to class. I had twenty extra books and several boxes of sharpened pencils which they could borrow. If they forgot to bring these materials, all they had to do was ask for a loan. I would not gnash my teeth or get red in the face; they would find me very willing to share my resources.

However, there was one catch. The borrowing student had to stand beside his desk (or lean over if written work was required) for that one-hour period. I smiled to myself in subsequent days as the kids raced around before class, trying to scrounge books or pencils from friends. Two hundred and twenty students came to my classroom every day, and yet I only had to enforce the 'standing' rule about once a week. The pupils watched out for their own best interests. One lapse in their memory was all it took; they didn't blunder into the same situation twice.

At the risk of being redundant, I will repeat the valuable formula for managing children and teenagers: give them maximum reason to comply with your wishes. Your anger is the *least* effective motivation I can imagine.

Q *If rewards and punishment should be given very quickly, why does God not interact that way with us, his children? People seem to 'get away' with bad behaviour for years, and the ultimate reward for those who live a Christian life will come only after death. Surely the Lord knows about 'immediate reinforcement'.*

A He certainly does. He created the characteristics we only observe and try to understand. So why does he no reinforce the behaviour he desires more quickly? I don't know, although that fact is acknowledged in Scripture:

> When the sentence for a crime is not quickly carried out, the hearts of the people are filled with schemes to do wrong. Although a wicked man commits a hundred crimes and still lives a long time, I know that it will go better with God-fearing men, who are reverent before God (Eccles 8:11–12, NIV).

Whether they arrive on time or not, the warnings and promises in Scripture are more reliable than anything else in the universe. He *will* have the last word!

Q *What is your opinion of the juvenile courts? Do they reward good behaviour and extinguish bad? Are they efficient in discouraging delinquency?*

A Not generally, but the blame is difficult to locate. I served for three years on President Ronald Reagan's National Advisory Commission to the Office of Juvenile Justice and Delinquency Prevention. It was a fascinating, although occasionally discouraging assignment. I observed that the courts build delinquents in some cases as systematically as if they were placing stone on stone.

This happened with a fourteen-year-old I knew who had broken every rule he could violate, just to demonstrate the toothlessness of the law. Craig would brag to his friends before committing an illegal act, and then laugh when he was not punished. In a matter of two years, he had stolen two cars and one motorcycle, had run away from home twice, was suspended from school three times, and was arrested once as a peeping Tom. I watched him march off to court repeatedly, where he was released after receiving another worn-out lecture from the judge.

Finally, Craig was sent to a camp for delinquent boys where he wrote me a letter saying how he regretted the mess he'd made of his life. He was anxious to get home and take advantage of his educational opportunity. I think Craig wanted to know how far he could push the law. As soon as he got the answer, he no longer wanted to fight. He should have been punished the first time he was arrested.

Shortly after hearing from Craig, I talked to a well-known judge about the obvious leniency of the courts. I asked him why juvenile authorities are so reluctant to take action against a defiant teenager, even though he may be begging for punishment. The judge cited two reasons for the attitudes of his colleagues:

First, there aren't enough correctional centres available for boys like Craig. Those that exist must be reserved for the greatest troublemakers.

Second, it is difficult for judges to get excited about milder forms of delinquency when they have been dealing with more serious cases involving murder, rape and robbery. It is unfortunate that the judges are limited in this fashion. A teenager's first encounter with the law should be so painful that he would not want to make the same mistake again, but our legal apparatus is not designed to accomplish that objective.

The juvenile courts occasionally commit the opposite error of dealing too harshly with a teenager. Such had been the case with Linda, a girl I met late one rainy afternoon. I was working on a report at my desk when I suddenly realised I was not alone. I looked up to see a barefoot, rain-soaked girl in my doorway. She was a pretty adolescent of about fifteen years.

'You can call the police now,' she instructed me.

'Why would I want to call the police?' I asked.

'Because I have run away.' She named a nearby detention home for delinquent girls. She said she'd spent the day hiding from the authorities.

She told me her name was Linda, and I asked her to sit down and tell me why she had run away. She started at the beginning, and I later verified the facts. Her mother had been a prostitute who gave no supervision or guidance to her daughter. Linda was even allowed to remain in the bedroom while her mother entertained men. The child was eventually taken away from her mother and made a ward of the court. She was placed in a home for young victims where there was not enough love to go around. Her mother came to see her for a few years, but then ignored her completely.

Linda was so starved of love that she ran away to find her mother. She was immediately returned to the home. A year later she tried to escape again, with the same result. Linda continued to run away, each time becoming more sophisticated in evading the police. The year before my introduction to this girl, she had vanished again, this time being picked up by several boys. They lived together for two weeks and were involved in several misdemeanours and various sexual escapades during that period.

Linda was subsequently arrested and brought before the juvenile court as a delinquent. She was sentenced to the detention centre for delinquent girls, surrounded by ten-foot chain link fences. The court considered her to be an unmanageable, incorrigible adolescent, yet this was wrong. Linda was a lonely, love-starved girl who had been cheated by the circumstances of life. She needed someone to care—not someone to punish. Perhaps the judge was too busy to study her background; perhaps he had no alternative place of care for Linda. Either way, the needs of this wispy girl remained unmet at this critical time of her life.

Juvenile justice must be designed to be lenient with the child who has been hurt, like Linda, and to sting the child who has challenged authority, like Craig. It is sometimes difficult to recognise the difference.

7

Discipline in Learning

When I was in college, there was a malicious little rumour going around that an amazing discovery had been made about human learning. A new technique called 'sleep teaching' made it possible to cram one's head full of facts while sleeping. I have to tell you that idea was very appealing to me. It would have fitted into my way of life perfectly to do the big-man-on-campus thing during the day and accomplish my studying while dreaming. Also, being a psychology student, I was interested in brain function and promptly set out to test the hypothesis.

I selected a class in which three tests were given during the term, with the lowest score being dropped by the lecturer. I studied hard for the first two exams and earned respectable marks, which permitted me to experiment with the third. When the exam was scheduled, I recorded all the necessary factual information on my tape recorder, being careful not to learn the detail as I spoke into the microphone. In all, about sixty minutes of data were packed on one side of an old reel-to-reel tape. Then I went out and enjoyed myself the night before the test. While my brighter friends were grinding away in the library, I was living it up in a restaurant with some guys who never studied much anyway. It felt wonderful.

At bedtime that night, I plugged the tape recorder into my clock radio so that my own voice would begin speaking to my unconscious mind at two o'clock in the morning. One hour later, I was awakened by the flopping of the tape at the end of the reel, and I reset the time for four o'clock. The tape played for another hour and awakened me again at five. The final 'hearing' occurred between six and seven. So passed the restless night.

The examination was scheduled for eight o'clock and I was there, yawning and bleary-eyed. The first thing I noted was that the questions on the printed exam sheet were not even vaguely familiar to me (always a bad sign). But I was still confident that the information was stored deep down in my brain, somewhere. I turned in the test and stood waiting for an invigilator to calculate my result. It only took a few minutes.

There were seventy-three people in the class, and I got the seventy-second-lowest marks. I managed to beat the class dummy by one point, but he appealed to the lecturer over a disputed answer and was granted two additional marks. I came in dead last! The only thing I got from the experiment was a terrible night's sleep and the wrath of a room-mate who had lain there in the moonlight learning rubbish he didn't want to know.

Many years have passed since those days of my callow youth when I still thought getting something for nothing was possible. I was dead wrong. Everything worth having comes with a price. The natural progression of the universe is movement from order to chaos, not the other way around. The only way to beat that curse is to invest energy into a project or objective. If improvement is to be made in anything, *especially* in the development of mental skills and knowledge, it will be accomplished through blood, sweat and a few tears. There's no way around it.

It is my belief that some, but by no means all, professional educators began to lose sight of that need for discipline in learning as we came through the turbulent sixties. They enthusiastically searched for an easier way to teach children than putting them through the rigours of structured classrooms, examinations, rules and requirements. Society was changing, authority went out of style, and all the traditional values began to look suspect. Why not throw out convention and try something new? How about—an 'open' classroom?

One of the most foolish ideas in the history of education was born. Let me cite excerpts from an article appearing in the *Seattle News Journal,* 27 May 1971, describing an open classroom in its full glory. Before doing so, however, let me emphasise that the excesses of the past are no longer evident in today's state schools. I'm hearing good things about the Seattle school district, for example, that experimented back in 1971 with the unstructured programme described below. If those days have past, then why do we focus on a time when schools went off at the deep end? Because we can't fully understand who we are today without examining where we've been. And because we can learn from the excesses of yesterday, when authority and discipline were distrusted. And because the remnants of this free-wheeling philosophy still lurk within our permissive society and the halls of academia.

The article referred to above was called 'The School Nobody Talks About', and was written by James and John Flaherty. As you read the following excerpts, imagine your own child enrolled in a programme of this nature.

Picture if you can, five- to twelve-year-olds riding tricycles down the school hall, painting on the walls, as they wish and what they wish, doing what they want to and when they want, communicating openly with their teachers in three- and four-letter words, dictating school policy, teaching, and curriculum as they wish. And all of this in a public [state] school in Seattle! Far out or impossible? No! It's happening right now in conservative old Seward Park. And the Seattle School District is picking up the tab.

The Elementary Alternative School is an experimental project of the school district. It began in November 1970 and was founded on the premise that regular elementary schools are too restrictive. It was cited that a school should teach the child to learn in a more natural environment and that his motivations to learn should arise from within himself. Also, that a child of any age is capable of making his own decisions and should be allowed to do so.

It's a kid's paradise. There is no formal curriculum, no age barriers, no classroom structure, no overall program. In fact, if the child doesn't want to learn the three Rs he doesn't have to.

On our tour, no formal classwork was being conducted. The children seemed to mill aimlessly in the three unkept classrooms. Apparently no class was in session. Then we entered the basement of the building next door . . . to consult with Mr. Bernstein (who directs the school). Bernstein . . . pointed out that this was a 'fully new concept in learning, as exemplified by A. S. Neill at Springhill, a progressive school in eastern U.S.' Bernstein said that four-letter words are often used to get attention or hammer home a point in his college classes, and he didn't see that it would harm any of the children in the Alternative School. 'You have to communicate with children in the language they understand,' he said.

Bernstein [was] queried on the fact that no formal classes were kept, no grades given, and therefore, how could a pupil finishing the sixth grade [aged eleven] enter a regular school. 'In six years,' Bernstein replied, 'perhaps all our schools will be like this one, and there'll be no problem.'

Not many school districts experimented with programmes as extreme as this one, fortunately, but the tenor of the times held authority and discipline in contempt. A depressing example of that changing philosophy was spelled out in a widely published book entitled *Summerhill*, by A. S. Neill, to whom Mr Bernstein referred. I was required to read this ridiculous book while doing postgraduate studies. It contradicted everything I believed about children, and indeed, about life itself. But Neill's writings and work were given great credibility in educational circles, and many teachers and head teachers (like Bernstein) were influenced by his laissez-faire philosophy.

Summerhill in England and Springhill in the USA were permissive institutions that conformed to the easy-come, easy-go philosophy of their director, A. S. Neill. Boarders were not required to get out of bed in the morning, attend classes, complete assignments, take baths, or even wear clothes. Rarely in human history have children been given wider latitude.

Let me list the elements of Neill's philosophy that governed his much-vaunted programme and which he recommended with great passion to parents the world over:

1. Adults have no right to insist on obedience from their children. Attempts to make the youngsters obey are merely designed to satisfy the adult's desire for power. There is no excuse for imposing parental wishes on children. They must be free. The best home situation is one where parents and children are perfect equals. A child should be required to do nothing until he *chooses* to do so. Neill went to great lengths to show the students that he was one of them—not their superior.

2. Children must not be asked to work at all until they reach eighteen years of age. Parents should not even require them to help with small errands or assist with the chores. We insult them by making them do our menial tasks. Neill actually stressed the importance of withholding responsibility from the child.

3. Religion should not be taught to children. The only reason religion exists in society is to release the false guilt it has generated over sexual matters. Our concepts of God, heaven, hell, and sin are based on myths. Enlightened generations of the future will reject traditional religion.

4. Punishment of any kind is strictly forbidden, according to Neill's philosophy. A parent who spanks his child actually hates him, and his desire to hurt the child results from his own unsatisfied sex life. At Summerhill, one young student broke seventeen windows without receiving so much as a verbal reprimand.

5. Adolescents should be told sexual promiscuity is not a moral issue at all. At Summerhill, premarital intercourse was not sanctioned only because Neill feared the consequences of public indignation. He and members of his staff sometimes went nude to eliminate sexual curiosity. He predicted that the adolescents of tomorrow would find a more healthy existence through an unrestricted sex life. (What they found was a disease called AIDS and a firsthand knowledge of other sexually transmitted diseases.)

6. No pornographic books or materials should be withheld from a child. Neill indicated that he would buy filthy literature for any of his students who wished to have it. This, he felt, would cure their prurient interests—without harming the child.

7. Children should not be required to say 'thank you' or 'please' to their parents. Further, they should not even be encouraged to do so.

8. Rewarding a child for good behaviour is a degrading and demoralising practice. It is an unfair form of coercion.

9. Neill considered books to be insignificant in a school. Education should consist largely of work with clay, paint, tools, and various forms of drama. Learning is not without value, but it should come after play.

10. Even if a child fails in school, the matter should never be mentioned by his parents. The child's activities are strictly his business.

11. Neill's philosophy, in brief, was as follows: eliminate all authority; let the child grow without outside interference; don't instruct him; don't force anything on him.

If A. S. Neill had been the only lonely proponent of this assault on authority, he would not have been worthy of concern. To the contrary, he represented an extreme example of a view that became very widely accepted in educational circles. Herbert R. Kohn wrote *The Open Classroom* and helped give respectability to a somewhat more sane version of the concept in American state schools. Believe it or not, this was 'cutting edge' stuff for more than a decade. We've now had twenty-five years to evaluate the fallout from the lessening of discipline and authority in the classroom. Look at what happened to the generation that was influenced most by it.

They concluded in the late sixties that God was dead, that immorality was the new morality, that disrespect and irreverence were proper, that unpopular laws were to be disobeyed, that violence was an acceptable vehicle for bringing change (as were their childhood tantrums), that authority was evil, that pleasure was paramount, that older people were not to be trusted, that diligence was distasteful, and that their country was unworthy of allegiance or respect. Every one of those components can be linked to the philosophy taught by A. S. Neill, but also believed by many of his contemporaries. It cost us a generation of our best and brightest, many of whom still suffer from the folly of their youth!

Not only did the misguided philosophy set up the student revolution of the late sixties. It also caused serious damage to our school system and the children who became the victims of it. I was a young teacher at the time and was shocked to see the lack of order and control in some of my colleagues' classrooms. The confusion was evident at every level. Tiny children in the reception class at primary school cowed their harassed teachers as systematically as did the boisterous secondary school students. In some situations, entire classes became so proficient at disrupting order that they were dreaded and feared by their future teachers. It seemed ridiculous for school officials to tolerate such disobedience when it could have been easily avoided. However, in instances when the educators did exercise firmness, many parents protested and demanded leniency for their children.

I have lived long enough now to have followed some of those kids into adult life. I've talked to them personally. I've read their testimonials. I've felt their anger. One of the most poignant statements I've seen was written in the 'My Turn' section of *Newsweek* magazine, 30 August 1976. The author, Myra Wolynski, was a product of the philosophy I have been describing. Her story, 'Confessions of a Misspent Youth', tells it all.

The idea of permissive education appealed to my mother in 1956 when she was a Bohemian and I was four. In Greenwich village, she found a small private school whose beliefs were hers and happily enrolled me. I know it was an act of motherly love but it might have been the worst thing she ever did to me. This school—I'll call it Sand and Sea—attracted other such parents, upper-middle-class professionals who were determined not to have their children pressured the way they had been. Sand and Sea was the school without pain. And it was the kind of school that the back-to-basics people rightly fear most. At Sand and Sea, I soon became an exemplar of educational freedom—the freedom not to learn.

Sand and Sea was run by fifteen women and one man who taught 'science'. They were decent people, some old, some young, and all devoted to cultivating the innate creativity they were convinced we had. There was a tremendous emphasis on the arts. We weren't taught techniques, however, because any kind of organization stunted creativity.

Happiness and Hieroglyphics. We had certain hours allotted to various subjects but we were free to dismiss anything that bored us. In fact, it was school policy that we were forbidden to be bored or miserable or made to compete with one another. There were no tests and no hard times. When I was bored with math, I was excused and allowed to write short stories in the library. The way we learned history was by trying to re-create its least important elements. One year, we pounded corn, made tepees, ate buffalo meat, and learned two Indian words. That was early American history. Another year we made elaborate costumes, clay pots, and papier-mâché gods. That was Greek culture. Another year we were all maidens and knights in armor because it was time to learn about the Middle Ages. We drank our orange juice from tin-foil goblets but never found out what the Middle Ages were. They were just 'The Middle Ages.'

I knew that the Huns pegged their horses and drank a quart of blood before going to war, but no one ever told us who the Huns were or why we should know who they were. And one year, the year of ancient Egypt, when we were building our pyramids, I did a thirty-foot-long mural for which I laboriously copied hieroglyphics onto the sheet of brown paper. But no one ever told me what they stood for. They were just there and beautiful.

Ignorance Is Not Bliss. We spent great amounts of time being creative because we had been told by our incurably optimistic mentors that the way to be happy in life was to create. Thus, we didn't learn to read until we were in the third grade, because early reading was thought to discourage creative spontaneity. The one thing they taught us very well was to hate intellectuality and anything connected with it. Accordingly, we were forced to be creative for nine years.

And yet Sand and Sea has failed to turn out a good artist. What we did do was to continually form and re-form interpersonal relationships, and that's what we thought learning was all about, and we were happy. At ten, for example, most of us were functionally illiterate, but we could tell that Raymond was 'acting out' when, in the middle of what passed for English, he did the twist on top of his desk. Or that Nina was 'introverted' because she always cowered in the corner.

When we finally were graduated, however, all the happy little children fell down the hill. We felt a profound sense of abandonment. So did our parents. After all that tuition money, let alone the loving freedom, their children faced high school with all the glorious prospects of the poorest slum-school kids. And so it came to be. No matter what school we went to, we were the underachievers and the culturally disadvantaged.

For some of us, real life was too much—one of my oldest friends from Sand and Sea killed himself two years ago after flunking out of the worst high school in New York at twenty. Various others have put in time in mental institutions where they were free, once again, to create during occupational therapy.

During my own high-school years, the school psychologist was baffled by my lack of substantive knowledge. He suggested to my mother that I be given a battery of psychological tests to find out why I was blocking out information. The thing was, I wasn't blocking because I had no information to block. Most of my Sand and Sea classmates were also enduring the same kinds of hardships that accompany severe handicaps. My own reading comprehension was in the lowest eighth percentile, not surprisingly. I was often asked by teachers how I had gotten into high school. However, I did manage to stumble not only through high school but also through college (first junior college—rejected by all four-year colleges, and then New York University), hating it all the way as I had been taught to. I am still amazed that I have a B.A., but think of it as a B.S.

The Lure of Learning. The parents of my former classmates can't figure out what went wrong. They had sent in bright, curious children and gotten back, nine years later, helpless adolescents. Some might say that those of us who freaked out would have freaked out anywhere, but when you see the same bizarre behavior pattern in succeeding graduating classes, you can draw certain terrifying conclusions.

Now I see my twelve-year-old brother (who is in a traditional school) doing college-level math and I know that he knows more about many other things besides math than I do. And I also see traditional education working in the case of my fifteen-year-old brother (who was summarily yanked from Sand and Sea, by my reformed mother, when he was eight so that he wouldn't become like me). Now, after seven years of real education, he is making impressive film documentaries for a project on the Bicentennial. A better learning experience than playing Pilgrim for four and a half months, and Indian for four and a half months, which is how I imagine they spent this year at Sand and Sea.

And now I've come to see that the real job of school is to entice the student into the web of knowledge and then, if he's not enticed, to drag him in. I wish I had been.

It was noble of the *Newsweek* publishers to print this emotional 'confession' by Myra Wolynski. After all, the popular press has been a significant part of the problem, extolling the virtues of avant-garde trends in the classroom. *Newsweek* magazine, for example, devoted its 3 May 1971 cover story to the topic, 'Learning Can Be Fun'. On the cover was a primary school girl making something with papier-mâché. Four years later, *Newsweek's* cover story considered 'Why Johnny Can't Write'. I wrote to the senior editor of *Newsweek* after the second article appeared, 8 December 1975, and suggested that maybe there was a link between the two stories. Perhaps Johnny couldn't write because he spent too much time having fun in the classroom. I received no reply.

Please understand, I am a supporter of the arts in the curriculum, and I certainly want the educational process to be as exciting and as much fun as possible. But children will not learn reading, writing and maths by making papier-mâché. And many of them will not pay the price to learn anything unless they are required to do so! Some educators have disagreed with this understanding and postulated that children will sweat and study because they have an inner thirst for knowledge.

A former director of public instruction in the state of California is quoted as saying:

> To say that children have an innate love of learning is as muddle-headed as to say that children have an innate love of baseball. Some do. Some don't. Left to themselves, a large percentage of the small fry will go fishing, pick a fight, tease the girls, or watch Superman on [TV]. Even as you and I!

It is a valid observation. Most of the time students will not invest one more ounce of effort in their studies than is required, and that fact has frustrated teachers for hundreds of years. Our schools, therefore, must have enough structure and discipline to *require* certain behaviour from their students. This is advantageous not only for academic reasons, but because one of the purposes of education is to prepare the young for later life.

To survive as an adult in this society, one needs to know how to work, how to get there on time, how to get along with others, how to stay with a task until completed, and, yes, how to submit to authority. In short, it takes a good measure of self-discipline and control to cope with the demands of modern living. Maybe one of the greatest gifts a loving teacher can contribute to an immature child, therefore, is to help him learn to sit when he feels like running, to raise his hand when he feels like talking, to be polite to his neighbour, to stand in line without smacking the kid in front, and to do language arts when he feels like doing football.

Likewise, I would hope to see more schools readopt reasonable dress codes, eliminating suggestive clothing, T-shirts with profanity or those promoting heavy metal bands, and so on. Guidelines concerning good grooming and cleanliness should also be enforced.

I know! I know! These notions are so alien to us now that we can hardly imagine such a thing. But the benefits would be apparent immediately. Admittedly, hair styles and matters of momentary fashion are of no particular significance, but adherence to a standard is an important element of discipline. The military has understood that for 5,000 years! If one examines the secret behind a top-of-the-league football team, a magnificent orchestra, or a successful business, the principal ingredient is invariably discipline. Thus, it is a great mistake to require nothing of children—to place no demands on their behaviour. We all need to adhere to some reasonable rules. How inaccurate is the belief that self-control is maximised in an environment which places no obligations on its children. How foolish is the assumption that self-discipline is a product of self-indulgence.

Before we leap to blame the educators for everything that has gone wrong, however, we need to take another look at the culture. The teachers and school administrators who guide our children have been among the most maligned and under-appreciated people in our society. They are an easy target for abuse. They are asked to do a terribly difficult job, and yet they are criticised almost daily for circumstances beyond their control. Some of their critics act as though educators are deliberately failing our kids. I strongly disagree. We would still be having serious difficulties in our schools if the professionals did everything right. Why? Because what goes on in the classroom cannot be separated from the problems occurring in society at large.

Educators certainly can't be blamed for the condition our kids are in when they arrive at school each day. It's not the teachers' fault that families are unravelling and that large numbers of their students have been sexually and/or physically abused, neglected, and undernourished. They can't keep kids from watching mindless television or 18-rated videos until midnight, or from using illegal substances or alcohol. In essence, when the culture begins to crumble from massive social problems that defy solutions, the schools will also look bad. That's why even though I disagree with many of the trends in modern education, I sympathise with the dedicated teachers and heads out there who are trying to do the impossible on behalf of our youngsters. They are discouraged today, and they need our support.

Still, there are steps that could be taken to reverse the errors of the past and create a more conducive climate for learning. At the secondary level, we can and *must* make schools a safer place for students *and* teachers. Knives, drugs and adolescence make a deadly cocktail. It is unbelievable what we have permitted to happen on school property. No wonder some kids can't think about their studies. Their *lives* are in danger! Yes, we can reduce the violence if we're committed to the task. Armed guards? Maybe. Metal detectors? If necessary. More expulsions? Probably. No-nonsense administrators? Definitely. Schools with strong leadership, like Joe Clark at Eastside High School in Paterson, New Jersey, have made dramatic progress in improving the academic environment. Above all, we must do what is required to pacify the combat zones in secondary schools.

We will not solve our pervasive problems, however, with the present generation of secondary school students. Our best hope long-term is to start over again with the youngsters just coming into primary school. We can rewrite the rules with these wide-eyed kids. Let's redesign the primary schools to include a greater measure of discipline. I'm not talking merely about more difficult projects and additional homework. I'm recommending more structure and control in the classroom. This is especially so in the United States, but applies to many schools in other parts of the world as well.

As the first official voice of the school, the primary teacher is in a position to construct positive attitudinal foundations on which future educators can build, or conversely, she can fill her young pupils with contempt and disrespect. A child's teachers during the first seven years will largely determine the nature of his attitude towards authority and the educational climate in secondary school (and beyond).

As indicated earlier, I taught in school for several years before completing my postgraduate studies and learned more about how children think from that daily exposure than could ever have been assimilated from a textbook. It was also enlightening to observe the disciplinary techniques utilised by other teachers. Some of them exercised perfect classroom control with little effort, while others faced the perpetual humiliation of student defiance. I observed that there was a fundamental difference in the way they approached their classes.

The unskilled teacher would stand in front of the boys and girls and immediately seek their affection. Although most good teachers want to be liked by their classes, some are very dependent on the acceptance of the children. On the first day of school in September, the new teacher, Miss Peach, gives the class a little talk which conveys this message: 'I'm so glad we had a chance to get together. This is going to be such a fun year for you; we're going to make soap, and soup, and we're going to paint a mural that will cover that entire wall. We'll take field trips and play games . . . this is going to be a great year. You're going to love me and I'm going to love you, and we'll just have a party.'

Her curriculum (within the general scope of the National Curriculum) is well saturated with fun, fun, fun activities, which are her tokens of affection to the class. All goes well the first day of school, because the children are a little intimidated by the start of a new academic year. But about three days later, little Butch is sitting over at the left and he wants to know what everyone else is questioning too: how far can we push Miss Peach? He is anxious to make a name for himself as a brave toughie, and he might be able to build his reputation at Miss Peach's expense.

At a well-calculated moment, he challenges her with a small act of defiance. Now the last thing Miss Peach wants is conflict, because she had hoped to avoid that sort of thing this year. She does not accept Butch's challenge; she pretends not to notice that he didn't do what she told him to do. He wins this first minor confrontation. Everyone in the class saw what happened: it wasn't a big deal, but Butch survived unscathed.

The next day, Matthew has been greatly encouraged by Butch's success. He defies her a little more openly than Butch did, and Miss Peach again ignores the challenge. From that moment forward, chaos begins to grow and intensify. Two weeks later Miss Peach is beginning to notice that things are not going very well. She's doing a lot of screaming each day and doesn't know how it got started; she certainly didn't intend to be an angry teacher. By February, life has become intolerable in her classroom; every new project she initiates is sabotaged by her lack of control. And then the thing she wanted least begins to happen: the students openly reveal their contempt for her. They call her names; they laugh at her weaknesses. If she has a physical flaw, such as a large nose or poor eyesight, they point this out to her regularly. Miss Peach cries quietly at break time, and her head throbs and pounds late into the night. The head teacher comes in and witnesses the anarchy, and he says, 'Miss Peach, you must get control of this class!' But Miss Peach doesn't know how to get control because she doesn't know how she lost it. It has been estimated that 80 per cent of the teachers in the USA who leave their jobs after the first year do so because of an inability to maintain discipline in their classroom.

Consider the contrasting approach of the skilful teacher, Mrs Justice. She wants the love of the class too, but she is more keenly aware of her responsibility to the children. On the first day of school she delivers her inaugural address, but it is very different from the one being spoken by Miss Peach. She says, in effect, 'This is going to be a good year, and I'm glad you are in my class. I want you to know that each one of you is important to me. I hope you will feel free to ask your questions, and enjoy learning in this class; I will not allow anyone to laugh at you, because it hurts to be laughed at. I will never embarrass you intentionally, and I want to be your friend. Well, we have some work to do so let's get started. Would you take out your maths books and turn to page 4.'

Mrs Justice just sounds like she knows what she's doing. Nevertheless, Butch's counterpart makes himself known about three days later. (There's at least one Butch in every classroom. If the troublemaker leaves during the year, a new demagogue will rise to take his place.) He challenges Mrs Justice in a small way, but she was not caught unprepared. She's been expecting him, and she socks it to him. He loses heavily! Everyone in the class gets the message: it doesn't pay to attack Mrs J. Poor Butch didn't do so well, did he?

Mrs Justice then delivers a little speech she has been saving for this moment. She says, 'There's something each of you should know. Your parents have given me the responsibility of teaching you some very important things this year, and I intend not to disappoint them. I have to get you ready for the things you will need to know next year. That's why I can't let one or two show-offs keep me from doing my job. Now, if you want to try to interfere with that purpose and disrupt what we're here to do, I can tell you it will be a miserable year for you. I have many ways to make you uncomfortable, and I will not hesitate to use them. Any questions? Good, let's get back to work.'

Mrs Justice then proceeds to follow a little formula that I favour tongue in cheek: don't smile till half-term. By then, this competent teacher has made her point. The class knows she's tougher, wiser and braver than they are. Here comes the good news: then they can begin to enjoy the pleasure of this foundation. She can loosen her control; the class can laugh together, talk together, and play together. But when she says, 'It is time to get back to work,' they do it because they know she is capable of enforcing her leadership. She does not scream. She does not hit. In fact, she can pour out the individual affection that most children need so badly. The class responds with deep love that will never be forgotten in those thirty-two lives. Mrs Justice has harvested the greatest source of satisfaction available in the teaching profession: awareness of profound influence on human lives.

Let me add, in conclusion, that there are tens of thousands of 'Mrs Justices' out there in state and private education today, who have put their lives on the line for their students. They should be among the most highly respected members of society because of their contribution to the development of human potential. Each of us can think back to teachers like Mrs J. in our earlier years who inspired us with a love of learning and helped make us who we are.

There are many men and women who hold this place of honour for me. I think of Mrs McAnally, my high school English teacher. She was tough as nails, but I loved her. I thought she was going to work me to death, but she taught me the fundamentals of grammar. She also taught me to keep my big mouth shut and listen to what I was told. In college and graduate school there were other strong lecturers who shaped and moulded my thinking: Dr Eddie Harwood, Dr Paul Culbertson, Dr C. E. Meyers, and Dr Ken Hopkins. With the exception of Dr Meyers who has died, all of these men are my good friends today. I owe them an unpayable debt.

In each case, however, their contributions to my life came through the avenue of *discipline*. Formal learning is impossible without it. The boring lecturers who asked and received nothing from me have been forgotten. The ones I remember today are those who invested themselves in me, and wouldn't take anything less than my best in return.

Does your child's school understand this necessity for structure, respect, commitment and discipline in the classroom? If so, why don't you call your child's teacher or the head and express your appreciation. They could use a pat on the back. Tell them you stand ready to assist in carrying out their important mission. If the school is not so oriented, get involved to help turn the tide. Meet with parent groups. Join the PTA. Work for the election of school governors who believe in traditional values and academic excellence. Schools function best when the time-honoured principle of local control—by parents—prevails. I believe it is making a comeback!

We'll pause now for a few more questions related to these unbiased and absolutely objective thoughts, and then look at a correlated aspect of discipline in learning.

Q *When Mrs Justice told her class that she had many ways to make her rebellious students uncomfortable, I would like to know what those things are.*

A If a school is committed to discipline and structure in the classroom, there are many things that Mrs Justice can do when challenged. Before I suggest a couple, let me say that the strong teacher rarely has to carry out a threat, just as a father who may be the stronger disciplinarian at home usually punishes less than the mother. There is something in the manner of a confident leader that says, 'Don't push me too far.' Some of it is convincing bluff. Some is in the way the first challenge is handled, as with Mrs Justice. And some is in the teacher's ability to express love to the child. Unfortunately, these are not skills that can be easily taught or reduced to a formula in a textbook. They *can* be learned somewhat from experience and from working with a good role model.

My wife, who was a wonderful teacher and a skilled manager of children, learned a new technique from another teacher who also taught a class of seven-year-olds in her school. This woman used an approach that was highly effective with the children. She spoke in very soft tones that forced them to listen very carefully in order to hear her. Somehow, she managed to infuse those thirty children with a quiet, orderly manner just by the way she led the class. Throughout the year, her room was rather like a public library where people whispered and moved quietly around the stacks. It was an impressive, God-given skill. Some have it. Some must work hard to acquire it.

Let me address the question more specifically now, considering those situations where disruptive students are tough and determined to force a showdown. What then? Everything depends on the age of the class, of course, but let me direct my answer at, say, eleven-year-olds. First, one must decide what is motivating the rebellious behaviour. Typically, the noisy kid seeks the attention of the group. Some children would much rather be thought of as obnoxious than to be unthought of at all. For them, anonymity is unacceptable. The ideal prescription is to extinguish their attention-getting behaviour and then meet their need for acceptance by less disruptive behaviour. An example may help.

I worked with a giddy little eleven-year-old named Larry whose mouth never shut. He perpetually disrupted the tranquility of his class, setting up a constant barrage of silliness, wisecracks and horseplay. His teacher and I constructed an isolation area in a remote corner of the schoolroom; from that spot he could see nothing but the front of the room. Thereafter, Larry was sentenced to a week in the isolation booth whenever he chose to be disruptive, which effectively eliminated the supporting reinforcement. Certainly, he could still act silly behind the screen, but he could not see the effect he was having on his peers, and they could not see him. Besides this limitation, each outburst lengthened his lonely isolation.

Larry spent one entire month in relative solitude before

the extinction was finalised. When he rejoined society, his teacher immediately began to reward his co-operation. He was given the high status jobs (as a messenger, and so on), and praised for the improvement he had made. The results were remarkable.

Sometimes these kinds of in-class responses to defiance do not work. Let's admit it. *Nothing* works for every child. In those cases, I have recommended an approach called 'systematic exclusion'. The parents are asked to come for a meeting and are made aware of the extreme behavioural problems that have developed. They are then informed that the only way for their child to remain in that school is for the student, the school, and the parents to enter into a three-party contract. It must be agreed that the mother or father will come to school and pick up the child if they are called during the school day. The child is told that he can come to school each morning, but the moment he breaks one of the well-defined rules, he will be sent home. No protests will be successful. He might be ejected for pushing other pupils in the queue at 9:01 am. Or he may make it until 1:15 or later before dismissal occurs. There are no second chances, although the child is free to return at the start of school the following morning. This would be a last resort before suspension.

Despite the common belief that children hate school, most of them hate staying at home even more. Daytime television gets pretty monotonous, particularly under the hostile eye of a mum who had to interrupt her activities to come to get her wayward son. Disruptive behaviour is sometimes quickly extinguished under this controlled setting. It just isn't profitable for the student to challenge the system. Positive reinforcement in the form of rewards is then generously applied for the child's attempts to learn and study.

I worked with another child in a behaviour modification classroom who was termed the most disruptive youngster ever seen at a major Los Angeles neuropsychiatric hospital. After four months in this controlled setting, he was able to attend a regular class in the state schools. *If* you can control the variables, you can usually influence behaviour.

Finally, let me return to the first comment I made in response to your question. Everything depends on the policy of the school. If the board and administration are committed to discipline and structure, control *can* be achieved. The teacher is not left to do battle with a room full of energetic, giggling, blabbing troops who outnumber him or her thirty-five to one. That classroom teacher is like a policeman in a squad car. He can call for backup any time he needs it, and no one blames him if that support is required.

Every teacher needs to know the head backs her in this way. Having been in the classroom myself, I can tell you I would not work in a school that didn't believe in discipline.

Q *Would you provide one more example of discipline in the classroom? Teachers need every technique they can get to reinforce their leadership these days. Describe a system that has worked.*

A Here's an idea that you might try. My wife, Shirley, taught in school for five years before resigning to have a baby. Several years after Danae was born, Shirley decided to teach part-time to help us support my expenses in the University of Southern California graduate school. The first thing she noticed when she went back to teaching was that it was much harder to control a class as a part-time teacher than as a full-time teacher.

'Oh boy!' shouted the kids when they saw her coming. 'We'll have fun today!'

Shirley and I sat down and discussed the struggles she was having with the children (aged seven to ten) she encountered each day. 'Loving them isn't enough,' she said. 'I need some leverage to keep them in order.'

We put our heads together and came up with a concept we called 'magic chalk'. This is how it worked. Shirley would get to the classroom early and draw a simple skull and cross-bones on the left side of the blackboard. Underneath were the words *Poison List*.

Beside the scary drawing she taped a single piece of paper. Then Shirley opened the doors and invited the children to come in. She did not, however, mention the skull as she pleasantly greeted her wide-eyed class. Within minutes, someone raised a hand to ask what everyone wanted to know: 'What's that picture there on the board?'

'Oh yes,' said Mrs Dobson. 'I meant to tell you about the poison list.'

'First,' she said, 'let me describe our class rules today.' She told them they would need to raise their hands before talking; to stay in their seats until given permission to leave, and to ask for help if they needed paper or to sharpen a pencil, and so on.

'Now, if you forget and break one of the rules, you will be asked to write your name on the board to the left of the poison symbol. Nothing will happen if you do. *But,* if you get your name on the board and then get two more marks by it—then (she said with ominous overtones) . . . *then* your name goes on the poison list. All I have to say to you is . . . *Don't* get your name on the poison list.' Shirley never quite told them what would happen to those unfortunate troops who made the big, bad list, but it *sounded* terrible. She hinted that it involved the head, but she never explained how.

Then Shirley quickly walked over to her desk where a brand-new piece of chalk sat in a cup on the edge of her desk.

'Does anyone know what this is?' she asked cheerfully.

'That's a piece of chalk,' several said at once.

'Not so!' replied Mrs Dobson. 'It may look like ordinary chalk, but it is much more important than that. This is *magic chalk*. Believe it or not, this little white stick has the ability to hear. It has tiny little ears right there on the side. It can also see you. Tiny eyes appear right there on the end.' (She had drawn them in.) 'The magic chalk is going to sit here on the edge of my desk, watching you and listening to what you say. It is looking for someone in particular. The magic chalk is hoping to see a boy or girl who is working very hard and being very quiet. And if it finds a student like that, it will suddenly appear on that person's desk.

'If you are the one chosen by the magic chalk, you do not have to ask what to do. Just pick it up, walk to the board and write your name over at the right side. Then for everyone chosen by the last class in the afternoon, you get a special treat.' (Are you ready for this?) 'You will be permitted to leave school three minutes early at the end of the day!'

Big deal? You bet it was. The three-minute factor was not so important in itself, but enjoying the status of being chosen by the chalk—writing your name on the board for all the world to see and then walking out of class when others had to stay—it was a treasure. There was also the thrill of having the chalk show up on one's desk, while others were working for the same goal.

The system worked like a charm because the kids loved it. In nearly two years of application every time Shirley was in the classroom, she usually managed to include most boys' and girls' names on the magic chalk list. But in all that time, she never once got a child's name on the poison list.

I consider this approach to have had all the ingredients of a well-designed system of discipline. First, it was fun for the kids. Second, it offered something to gain for doing things right and something to lose for misbehaving. Third, it required no anger on the part of the teacher. And fourth, it was easy to implement.

Use your creativity to design a scheme for yourself. Children up to the age of eleven love games, fantasies and contrived symbols or status. Older students are remarkably tougher to entice.

Q *Did any parent or administrator complain about Shirley's use of the symbol of death, or about having the children unsupervised three minutes early? And what about associating a child with poison—a deadly substance?*

A No one ever criticised the system, to my knowledge, although they certainly *could* have. *Any* system of discipline will be opposed by some people today. Whether misbehaving children are kept after school ('The day is long enough already') or made to write sentences 100 times ('What a waste of effort—there's no learning in it'), or if really troubled kids are suspended from school ('Philosophically we're opposed to it'), there is no method of controlling children that won't draw fire from *someone.* I think, however, that teachers should be given a little latitude for the common good. Otherwise, chaos will reign in the classroom.

Q *Myra Wolynski said in her 'Confession' article that Sand and Sea would not allow classroom organisation or structure because it damaged creativity. I have heard that view expressed many times. Can it be supported?*

A We've all heard the warning that firm discipline destroys creativity, and there have been some studies to validate that assumption. However, it seems to me that creativity can flourish only when there's enough order to allow for concentrated thought. Chaos and creativity don't mix. On the other hand, an extremely oppressive atmosphere also stifles learning, which is what the research demonstrates. Everything seems to circle back to that word *balance,* which certainly has its place in the classroom.

Q *What would you do if you had a primary school child in a chaotic classroom with a disorganised teacher?*

A I would do everything I could to transfer my child to another class—though the final decision would of course rest with the head, and only rarely can children be moved.

Of course, if the situation seems really hopeless, you could switch to another school. Some very bad habits and attitudes can develop in ten months with an incompetent role model.

Q *You seem to favour a teaching method that emphasises the memorisation of specific facts, which I consider to be a very low level of learning. We need to teach concepts to our kids and help them learn how to think—not just fill their heads with a bunch of details.*

A I agree that we want to teach concepts to students, but that does not occur in a vacuum. For example, we would like them to understand the concept of the solar system and how the planets are positioned in rotation around the sun. How is that done? One way is for them to learn the distances between the heavenly bodies, ie, the sun is 93 million miles from earth, but the moon is only 240,000. The concept of relative positions is then understood from the factual information. What I'm saying is that an understanding of the right factual information can and should lead to conceptual learning.

Q *But again, you're putting too much emphasis on the memorisation process, which is a low academic goal.*

A The human brain is capable of storing some 2,000 million bits of information in the course of a lifetime. There are many avenues through which that programming can occur, and memorisation is one of them. Let me put it this way. If you ever have to go under a surgeon's knife, you'd better hope that he has memorised—I said memorised—every muscle, every bone, every blood vessel, and every Boy Scout knot in the book. Your life will depend on his accessibility to factual information during the operation. Obviously, I strongly oppose the perspective held in some academic circles that says, 'There's nothing we know for certain so why learn anything?' Those who feel that way have no business teaching. They are salesmen with nothing to sell!

Q *Like you, I have observed that schoolchildren—even the older ones—tend to admire the stricter teachers. Why is this true?*

A Teachers who maintain order are often the most respected members of the staff, provided they aren't mean and bad tempered. One who can control a class without being oppressive is almost always loved by her students. That is true because there is safety in order. When a class is out of control, particularly at the primary school level, the children are afraid of each other. If the teacher can't make the class behave, how can she prevent a bully from doing his thing? How can she keep the children from laughing at one of the less able members? Children are not very fair and reasonable with each other, and they feel good about having a strong teacher who is.

Second, children love justice. When someone has violated a rule, they want immediate retribution. They admire the teacher who can enforce an equitable legal system, and they find great comfort in reasonable social expectations. By contrast, the teacher who does not control her class inevitably allows crime to pay, violating something basic in the value system of children.

Third, children admire strict teachers because chaos is nerve-racking. Screaming and hitting and wiggling are fun for about ten minutes; then the confusion begins to get tiresome and irritating.

I have smiled in amusement many times as seven- and eight-year-olds astutely evaluated the relative disciplinary skills of their teachers. They know how a class should be conducted. I only wish all of their teachers were equally aware of this important attribute.

Q *Can you give us a guideline for how much work children should be given to do?*

A There should be a healthy balance between work and play. Many farm children of the past had daily chores that made life pretty difficult. Early in the morning and again after school they would feed the pigs, gather the eggs, milk the cows, and bring in the wood. Little time was reserved for fun, and childhood became a pretty drab experience. That was an extreme position, and I certainly don't favour its return.

However, contrast that level of responsibility with its opposite, recommended by Neill, where we shouldn't even ask our children to mow the lawn or let out the cat. According to this recommendation, our child should be allowed to lie on his over-fed stomach watching six or eight hours of worthless television while his schoolwork gathers dust in the corner. Both extremes, as usual, are harmful to the child. The logical middle ground can be found by giving the child an exposure to responsibility and work, but preserving time for his play and fun. The amount of time devoted to each activity should vary with the age of the child, gradually requiring more work as he grows older.

A final thought

As we conclude this discussion of discipline in learning, I would like to return to an interview published in the first edition of *Dare to Discipline*. It was originally printed in *U.S. News & World Report,* April 1965, and featured world renowned criminologists, Professor and Mrs Sheldon Glueck.[1] The Gluecks are most noted for their longitudinal study of juvenile delinquency and its causes. Note how prophetic their words were as they described the teenagers of their day and where society appeared to be moving.

U.S. News: *What seems to be causing delinquency to grow so fast nowadays?*

Glueck: There are many causes for this. For the most part, however, what we are seeing now is a process that has been going on since the second World War.

First, you have more and more mothers going to work. Many have left their children more or less unattended, at home or on the streets. This has deprived children of the constant guidance and sense of security they need from their mothers in their early years.

Along with that change, parental attitudes toward disciplining their young have changed quite rapidly. In the home and outside, the trend has been steadily toward more permissiveness—that is, placing fewer restraints and limits on behavior.

U.S. News: *How has that philosophy worked out in practice?*

Glueck: Not very well, it seems. Life requires a certain amount of discipline. You need it in the classroom, you need it in the home, you need it in society at large. After all, the Ten Commandments impose a discipline. *Unless general restraints are built into the character of children, you can arrive eventually at social chaos.*

U.S. News: *Are you saying that moral values are crumbling? (Author's note: This question preceded the so-called 'new morality' by several years.)*

Glueck: This is part of the picture. Not only parents, but others are uncertain in many cases as to what is morally right or wrong, and that makes discipline harder to enforce.

For instance, children today are being exposed to all kinds of moving pictures and books. It is difficult to decide what moving pictures and books should be censored.

In a broad sense, actually, you might feel that censorship in general is undesirable. Yet you also know that restraint must be imposed at some point—especially where children are involved. But in trying to decide at what point restraint should be imposed, it very often turns out that no restraint at all results. And it is this lack of restraint in the home and on the outside that is back of so much of our delinquency.

U.S. News: *Do juvenile courts tend to be too soft on youngsters?*

Glueck: Sometimes, yes, but more often there is inconsistency because judges have wide discretion; and they may rely on intuition and hunches rather than the use of predictive data which their staff could gather for them on each case.

U.S. News: *Then is stern punishment a deterrent to further crime?*

Glueck: Certainty of punishment is definitely a deterrent. After all, fear is a primary emotion in man. It plays an important part in his training. We have gone rather far in the other direction, in letting the child feel that he isn't going to be punished for his misdeeds.

Of course, it is wrong to rely exclusively on fear of punishment, but it is equally wrong to do away with this deterrent.

U.S. News: *Can schools help in keeping children from developing into troublemakers?*

Glueck: They certainly can. As we have said, there are children whose energies are not suited to long periods of sitting still and whose adventuresomeness has to be satisfied in some acceptable way.

We also think that one of the basic needs of schools, along with other elements of society, is a general recognition that rules must be observed—that, without rules, you drift into chaos and tyranny and into taking the law into your own hands. You see it not only among delinquents, but among young college students, in their demand for more and more freedom from restraints and from higher authority.

U.S. News: *Do you look for crime and delinquency to grow?*

Glueck: Probably. Our own feeling is that, *unless much is done to check the vicious cycles involved, we are in for a period of violence beyond anything we have yet seen.*

All you have to do is to read about the murders and assaults taking place in New York subways. Only a few years ago nobody thought of public conveyances as being unsafe. *We foresee no letup in this trend.* A delinquent child often grows up to produce delinquent children—not as a matter of heredity, but of his own unresolved conflicts which make him an ineffective parent.

Professor and Mrs Glueck clearly anticipated the anarchy that is now rumbling through the midsection of democracy. Isn't it time for us to address the root causes which the Gluecks recognised three decades ago?

8

The Barriers to Learning

PART 1

We have been discussing the importance of discipline in the parent-child relationship, particularly as concerned with obedience, respect and responsibility. We have also examined the importance of authority in the classroom. Now it is appropriate to examine another aspect of discipline: that dealing with the training of a child's mental faculties and moral character.

The primary concern will be with the thousands of children who do not succeed in school—the 'academic casualties' who cannot, or will not, carry the intellectual responsibility expected of them. Their parents cry and beg and threaten; their teachers push and shove and warn. Nevertheless, they sit year after year in passive resistance to the adult coercion. Who are these youngsters for whom academic discipline seems so difficult? Are they lazy? Are they unintelligent? Do they care? Are our teaching methods ineffective? How can we help them avoid the sting of failure in these early experiences?

During my years of service as a school psychologist, I was impressed by the similarities in the students who were referred to me with learning problems. Although each child was an individual with unique characteristics, the majority of failing youngsters shared certain kinds of problems. There were several sets of circumstances which repeatedly interfered with disciplined learning in the classroom. In this chapter and the next, I will describe the three major categories of children who do poorly in school. Parents should look closely for the footprints of their own children.

The late developer

Donald is five years old and will soon go to school. He is an immature little fellow who is still his mummy's baby in many ways. Compared to his friends, Donald's language is childish and he lacks physical co-ordination. He cries three or four times a day, and other children take advantage of his innocence. A developmental psychologist or a pediatrician would verify that Donald is neither physically nor mentally retarded; he is merely progressing on a slower physiological timetable than most children his age.

Nevertheless, Donald's fifth birthday has arrived, and everyone knows that five-year-olds go to school. He is looking forward to it, but deep inside he is rather tense about this new challenge. He knows his mother is anxious for him to do well in school, although he doesn't really know why. His father has told him he will be a 'failure' if he doesn't get a good education.

He's not certain what a failure is, but he is sure he doesn't want to be one. Mum and Dad are expecting something outstanding from him and he hopes he won't disappoint them. His sister Pamela is in her second year now; she is doing well. She can read and print her letters and she knows the names of every day in the week. Donald hopes he will learn those things too.

On the first day of term, Donald clutches his Mickey Mouse lunch box and walks on wobbly legs to the reception class. From day one he has academic trouble, and reading seems to be his biggest source of difficulty. His teacher, Miss Fudge, introduces the alphabet to her class, and Donald realises that most of his friends have already learned it. He has a little catching up to do. But too quickly Miss Fudge begins teaching something new. She wants the class to learn the sounds each letter represents, and soon he is even further behind.

Before long, the class begins to read stories about interesting things. Some children can zing right along, but Donald is still working on the alphabet. Miss Fudge divides the class into three reading groups according to their initial skill. She wants to conceal the fact that one group is doing more poorly than the others, so she gives them the camouflage names of 'Lions', 'Tigers' and 'Giraffes'. Miss Fudge's motive is noble, but she fools no one. It takes the children about two minutes to realise that the Giraffes are all stupid! Donald begins to worry about his lack of progress, and the gnawing thought looms that there may be something drastically wrong with him.

During the first parent-teacher meeting in October, Miss Fudge tells Donald's parents about his problems in school. She describes his immaturity and his inability to concentrate or sit still in the classroom. He's out of his seat most of the day.

'Nonsense,' says his father. 'What the child needs is a

little drill.' He insists that Donald bring home his books, allowing father and son to sit down for an extended academic exercise. But everything Donald does irritates his father. His childish mind wanders and he forgets the things he was told five minutes before. As his father's tension mounts, Donald's productivity descends. At one point, Donald's father crashes his hand down on the table and bellows, 'Would you just pay attention and stop being so STUPID!' The child will never forget that cutting assessment.

Whereas Donald struggled vainly to learn during his early days in school, by November he has become disinterested and unmotivated. He looks out of the window. He draws and doodles with his pencil. He whispers and plays. Since he can't read, he can neither spell nor write. He is uninvolved and bored, not knowing what is going on most of the time. He feels weird and inadequate.

'Please stand, Donald, and read the next paragraph,' says his teacher. He stands and shifts his weight from foot to foot as he struggles to identify the first word. The girls snigger and he hears one of the boys say, 'What a twit!' The problem began as a developmental lag, but has now become an emotional time bomb and a growing hatred for school.

Unfortunately, a child's age is the *worst* possible criterion on which to determine the beginning of his school career. Five-year-old children vary tremendously in their degree of maturity. Some are precocious and wise, while others are mere babies like Donald. Furthermore, the development of boys tends to be about six months behind girls at this age. As can be seen, a slow-maturing boy who turns five right before school starts is miles behind most of his peers. This immaturity has profound social and intellectual implications.

One reason an immature child does poorly in school may be related to the absence of an organic substance called myelin. At birth, the nervous system of a body is not insulated. An infant is unable to reach out and grasp an object because the electrical command or impulse is lost on its journey from the brain to the hand. Gradually, a whitish substance (myelin) begins to coat the nerve fibres, allowing controlled muscular action to occur.

Myelinisation proceeds from the head downwards (cephalocaudal) and from the centre of the body outwards (proximodistal). In other words, a child can control the movement of his head and neck before the rest of his body. Control of the shoulder precedes the elbow, which precedes the wrist, which precedes the large muscles in the hands, which precedes small muscle co-ordination of the fingers.

Schoolchildren are usually taught to print their letters first before they learn cursive writing because of the delayed development of minute finger control. This development pattern is critically important to the late developer. Since the visual apparatus in humans is usually among the last neural mechanisms to be myelinated, the immature child may not have undergone this necessary development process by the time he is five.

A child who is extremely immature and unco-ordinated may be neurologically unprepared for the intellectual tasks of reading and writing. Reading, particularly, is a highly complex neurological process. The visual stimulus must be relayed to the brain without distortion where it should be interpreted and retained in the memory. Not all five-year-olds are equipped to perform this task. Unfortunately, however, our culture permits few exceptions or deviations from the established timetable. A five-year-old must learn to read or else face the emotional consequences of failure.

The question may be asked, 'Why doesn't the late developer catch up with his class when he matures in subsequent years?' If the problem were simply a physical phenomenon, the slow maturing child could be expected to gain on his early developing friends. However, emotional factors are invariably tangled in this difficulty.

The self-image is amazingly simple to damage but exceedingly difficult to reconstruct. Once a child begins to think he's stupid, incapable, ignorant, or foolish, the concept is not easily eliminated. If he falters in the early academic setting, he is squeezed by the vice-like demands at school and expectations at home. The emotional pressure is often unresolvable. There is no rationalisation he can give parents and teachers to explain his perceived failure. Nor is there a balm they can offer which will soothe his damaged psyche. His self-concept is often wounded by this tension, and his personality will probably reflect the experience well into adult life.

The solution for late developers is relatively simple: instead of scheduling the child's entrance into school according to his age, the optimal timetable should be determined by neurological, psychological, social and pediatric variables. A simple screening test could identify extreme cases, such as Donald. The majority of children could begin school at five, although more flexibility would be reserved for the exceptional child.

Regardless of the school's adoption or rejection of this

recommendation, I would suggest that parents of an immature youngster have him examined for educational readiness by a child development specialist (child psychologist or pediatrician). This procedure should be a 'must' for slow-maturing boys for whom birthdays occur late in the academic year. The consequences of doing this cannot be underestimated. This simple procedure may spare your child many years of grief.

If it is determined that the child is a late developer, I believe he should repeat the reception class. In the United States, he can even stay at home another year. Despite common wisdom on this issue children in America who are home-schooled in the first few years of primary school do not tend to be maladjusted or handicapped when they re-enter formal education. Nor are they 'unsocialised'. If parents are willing to bring the at-home child into their world, talking to them and allowing them to go to the shops, take field trips, help cook and work in the garage with Dad, they do not need hour upon hour of formal desk work.[1] Research on this issue has been specific and most encouraging.[2]

What happens, then, when the time for re-entry occurs? In most cases, those home-schooled kids catch up and pass their classmates in a matter of months. They're also inclined to be leaders in years to come[3] because they haven't been bludgeoned in the early days of vulnerability. In other words, they are less peer-dependent.[4]

If that seems strange, remember that Jesus didn't 'go to school' until he was twelve years old. That was the custom in Israel in those days. Formal classwork for the immature child, and indeed, even for the go-getter, is simply not necessary at the very young ages. I know this fact contradicts what the education authorities would like us to believe; they recommend mandatory education for all above four years old. It is also unpopular among parents who have two-career families and need some safe wholesome place for their children. But that effort to take children out of the home at an earlier age simply will not conform to the realities of child development.

This is why the home-schooling movement is growing by leaps and bounds in the States. Our organisation, Focus on the Family, recently polled a random sample of 4,000 constituents to see what trends and opinions were evident among them. To our surprise, 13 per cent were involved in home schooling. Though challenging for mothers (and fathers), this approach to the education of the next generation has been highly successful. It is especially appropriate for kids like Donald, who need some time to grow up before formal classwork begins.

At the time I first wrote *Dare to Discipline,* I had never heard of home schooling. I had been taught in graduate school to believe in the value of earlier and earlier formal classroom experience. Now, I am an enthusiastic supporter of keeping kids with their parents for a longer time. Dr Raymond Moore, author of *School Can Wait* and an early leader of the home-schooling movement, had a great influence on me in the early eighties. Admittedly, home schooling is not for everyone, but it has been highly successful for most who have tried it. I will say this: if Shirley and I had it to do over again, we would have home schooled our two children, at least for the first few years!

The law states that a reasonable level of education must be maintained for all children, and rightly so. If you can't home school your child, or allow him to repeat his first year, I strongly recommend that he be spared academic pressure until he can get his spindly legs stabilised beneath his body.

The slow learner

The 'slow learner' is another youngster likely to have great trouble with academic discipline, resulting from his inability to learn as quickly as his peers. Before going further, I must ask the reader to endure a brief technical explanation at this point. To understand slow learners, we must refer to the normal distribution of intelligence quotients representing the general population.

The area in the centre of the distribution represents the 'normal range' of IQ scores, which fall between 90 and 110. The precise IQ points for each category vary according to the standard deviation of the intelligence test utilised. Fifty per cent of all individuals score within this middle area on most tests of intelligence. It is interesting to note that virtually everyone thinks his IQ is above 100. If we asked 10,000 people to estimate their expected level of ability, very few would guess an IQ score below average. The fact is, half the total population would actually score below 100.

Likewise, parents will often ascribe fantastic intelligence quotients to their children. A familiar but comical remark is 'Herbert has an IQ of 214, according to a test he took in the Sunday supplement.' *Very* few individuals score above 150, and Herbert is not likely to be one of them.

The 'gifted' individuals are represented at the far right of the distribution. Approximately 2 per cent of all children and adults have this exceptionally bright level of ability. By contrast, nearly 3 per cent of the population appears at the other end of the intellectual continuum, and are referred to as 'retarded'. All local education authorities provide special education for children with learning difficulties, and some offer special facilities for the gifted.

As indicated, the purpose of presenting these facts is to highlight the problems of the slow learners—those children having IQs between 70 and 90. These students comprise nearly one-fourth of the children in a typical school. In many ways, they are the saddest youngsters with whom child development specialists deal. Of particular concern are the individuals with IQs in the lower range of the slow learner classification (70 to 80) who are virtually destined to have difficulties in school. No special education is available for them, *although they are not appreciably different from the borderline retarded students.*

In America, a retarded child with an IQ of 70 would

probably qualify for highly specialised and expensive educational programmes, including a smaller class, specially trained teacher, audio visual aids and a 'no fail' policy. By contrast, a slow learning child with an IQ of 80 would usually receive no such advantages. He must compete in regular classes against the full range of more capable students. Such competition implies winners and losers, and it is the slow learner who invariably 'loses'.

Let's consider the plight of the unintelligent young child in the classroom. Here is the child who 'would if he could—but can't'. He rarely, if ever, experiences the thrill of getting good marks on his spelling test. He is the last child chosen in any academic game or contest. He often has the *least* sympathy from his teachers. He is no more successful in social activities than academic pursuits, and the other children reject him openly.

Like the late developer, the slow learner gradually develops a crushing image of failure that distorts his self-concept and damages his ego. This was exemplified by a conversation overheard by a colleague of mine between two intellectually handicapped students. Discussing their prospects with girls, one of them said, 'I do okay until they find out I'm a retard.' Obviously, this child was keenly aware of his inadequacy.

There is no better way to assassinate self-confidence in our children than to place 25 per cent of them in a situation where excellence is impossible to achieve, where inadequacy is the daily routine, and where inferiority is a living reality. It is not surprising that such a child is often a mischievous tormentor at eight, a bully at eleven, a loudmouth in the first years of secondary school and a drop-out/delinquent later on.

The slow learner is unlike the late developer in one major respect: time will not resolve his deficiency. He will not do better next year. In fact, he tends to get further behind as he grows older.

What can be done for these children? Listed below are the steps that could tip the scales in favour of this vast number of youngsters.

1. *Teach them to read, even if a one-to-one teacher-student ratio is required (and it probably will be).* Nearly every child can learn to read, but *many* children have difficulty if taught only in large groups. Their minds wander and they do not ask questions as readily. It would be expensive for the school to support additional remedial reading teachers, but no expenditure would be more helpful. Special techniques, teaching machines, and individual reinforcement can be successful in teaching this most basic skill to children who are least likely to learn without individual attention. This assistance should *not* be delayed until the child is nine or ten, or in secondary school. By then the slow learner has already endured the indignities of failure.

Many schools in the States have implemented creative programmes to focus on reading problems. One such programme, the 'ungraded primary', eliminates distinctions between students in the first three grades. Instead of grouping children by age, they are combined according to reading skill. Good readers in the first, second and third grades may occupy the same classes. Poor readers are also grouped together. This procedure takes the sting out of retention and allows slow learners to benefit from homogeneous grouping.

Another popular system is called the 'split reading'

programme. In this method, the better half of readers in a class arrives at school thirty minutes early for specialised instructions. The slower half remains half an hour later each day for the same purpose.

There are many such programmes to teach reading more effectively. Parents who are concerned about their child's basic academic skills may wish to seek tutorial assistance to supplement these school programmes.

2. *The slow learner should be shielded from the devastation of failure.* Scholastic goals which the slow learner can't attain should be de-emphasised. He should be required to do only things that are within his reach. He should be praised when he does his best, even if his work isn't on par with his peers. The slow learner is entitled to self-acceptance too, even in this fast-paced technological world.

3. *Remember that success breeds success.* The best motivation for a slow learner is to know he is succeeding. If adults in his life show confidence in him, he will more likely have confidence in himself. In fact, most humans share this characteristic. We tend to act the way we think other people 'see' us.

I learned this when I joined the National Guard at twenty-two years of age. I had recently graduated from college and had already been accepted into graduate school. Thus, I enlisted for extended reserve duty in the military rather than serve two years' active duty. I was immediately packed on a bus for Fort Ord, California, to undergo a six-month basic training and army administrative course. Contrary to the recruiting posters, this exciting new career opportunity was not a matter of personal choice; it was selected for me. Nevertheless, I spent the next six months learning the fascinating world of military forms, typing and filing. It bored me silly.

One hundred and eighty-three days later I returned to the local National Guard unit with this newly acquired knowledge available for usage. Surprisingly, I was not welcomed back with much enthusiasm. That's because I was a private and everyone knows privates are stupid. I was outranked by practically the whole world—so it stood to reason there was thickness between my ears. Everybody from the privates-first-class to the colonel anticipated ignorant behaviour from me. To my amazement, their expectation proved accurate.

My first assignment after those months of office training was to type a simple letter in two copies. After twenty-five minutes of concentrated effort, I realised the carbon paper, used in those days, was back to front. Reverse lettering was smudged all over the back of the main copy, which did not ingratiate me with the sergeant. Similar complex procedures, like remembering regulations, were strangely difficult to perform. Looking back, it is clear that *my performance was consistent with my image.*

I then went into a tough graduate school programme and earned a PhD. Self-image was the difference.

Likewise, many children who fail in school are merely doing what they think others expect of them. Our reputation with our peers is a very influential force in our lives. This is especially true of slow learners, who represent one-quarter of all students. Perhaps your child is one of them.

In the next chapter, we'll follow the footprints of the third type of child for whom academic discipline seems so difficult. Stay tuned.

Q *If age is such a poor factor to use in determining the start of school why is it applied so universally in our country?*

A Because it is so convenient. Parents can plan for the definite beginning of school when their child turns five. School officials can survey their districts and know how many school entrants they will have the following year. If an eight-year-old moves into the area in October, the administrator knows which class the child will go into, and so on. The use of chronological age as a criterion for school entrance is great for everybody—except the late developer.

Q *What causes a child to be a slow learner?*

A There are many hereditary, environmental and physical factors which contribute to one's intellect, and it is difficult to isolate the particular influences. Accumulating evidence seems to indicate that some slow learning and even borderline retardation is caused by a lack of intellectual stimulation in the child's very early years. There appears to be a critical period during the first three to four years when the potential for intellectual growth must be seized. There are enzyme systems in the brain that must be activated during this brief window. If the opportunity is missed, the child may never reach his capacity.

Children who grow up in deprived circumstances are more likely to be slow learners. They may not have heard adult language regularly. They have not been provided with interesting books and puzzles to occupy their sensory apparatus. They have not been taken to the zoo, the airport, or other exciting places. They have not received daily training and guidance from adults. This lack of stimulation may inhibit the brain from developing properly.

The effect of early stimulation on living brains has been studied in several fascinating animal experiments. In one, researchers divided litter-mate rats into two identical groups. The first group was given maximum stimulation during the first few months of life. These rats were kept in well-lit cages, surrounded by interesting paddle wheels and other toys. They were handled regularly and allowed to explore outside their cages. They were subjected to learning experiences and then rewarded for remembering. The second group lived the opposite kind of existence. These rats crouched in dimly lit, drab, uninteresting cages. They were not handled or stimulated in any way, and were not permitted outside their cages. Both groups were fed identical food.

At 105 days of age, all the rats were sacrificed to permit examination of their neurological apparatus. The researchers were surprised to find that the high stimulation rats had brains that differed in several important ways: (1) the cortex (the thinking part of the brain) was thicker and wider; (2) the blood supply was much more abundant; (3) the enzymes necessary for learning were more sophisticated. The researchers concluded that high stimulation experienced during the first group's early lives had resulted in more advanced and complex brains.

It is always risky to apply conclusions from animal research directly to humans, but the same kinds of changes probably occur in the brains of highly stimulated children. If parents want their children to be capable, they should begin by talking to them at length while they are still babies. Interesting mobiles and toys should be arranged around the cot. From then on through the toddler years, learning activities should be arranged regularly.

Of course, parents must understand the difference between stimulation and pressure. Providing books for a three-year-old is stimulating. Ridiculing and threatening him because he can't read them is pressuring. Imposing unreachable expectations can have a damaging effect on children.

If early stimulation is as important as it now appears, then the lack thereof may be a leading cause of slow learning and even mild retardation. It is imperative that parents take the time and invest their resources in their children. The necessity for providing rich, edifying experiences for young children has never been so obvious as it is today.

Q *I've read that it's possible to teach four-year-olds to read. Should I be working on this with my child?*

A If a youngster is particularly sharp and can learn to read without feeling undue adult pressure, it might be advantageous to teach him this skill. But that's a much bigger 'if' than most people realise. Few parents can work with their own children without showing frustration over natural failures. It's like teaching your wife to drive: risky at best, disastrous at worst!

Besides this limitation, learning should be programmed at the age when it is most needed. Why invest unending effort in teaching a child to read when he has not yet learned to cross the street, tie his shoes, count to ten, or answer the telephone? It seems foolish to get panicky over preschool reading as such.

The best policy is to provide your children with many interesting books and materials, read to them and answer their questions. Then let nature take its unobstructed course.

Q *Should schoolchildren be required to wear clothes which they dislike?*

A Generally not. Children are very concerned about the threat of being laughed at by their friends and will sometimes go to great lengths to avoid that possibility. Conformity is fuelled by the fear of ridicule. Teenagers particularly seem to feel, 'The group can't laugh at me if I am identical to them.' From this perspective, it's unwise to make a child endure unnecessary social humiliation. Children should be allowed to select their own clothes, within the obvious limits of budget, good taste and school guidelines.

Q *Do slow learners and mentally retarded children have the same needs for esteem that others have?*

A As I have explained elsewhere, I sometimes wish they didn't, but their needs are no different. During a portion of my early psychology training at Lanternman State Hospital in Pomona, California, I was impressed by the vast need for love shown by some of the most retarded patients. There were times when I would step into the door of a children's ward and forty or more severely retarded youngsters would rush towards me screaming

'Daddy! Daddy! Daddy!' They would push and shove around my legs with their arms held up, making it difficult to avoid falling. Their deep longing to be loved simply couldn't be satisfied in the group experiences of hospital life, despite the exceptionally high quality of care at Lanternman.[5]

The need for esteem has led me to favour a current trend in education, whereby borderline mentally retarded children are given special assistance *within* their regular classrooms without segregating them in special classes. The stigma of being a 'retard', as they call themselves, is no less insulting for a ten-year-old than it would be for you or me.

9

The Barriers to Learning

PART 2

As we saw in the previous chapter, thousands of children fall short of the standards expected of them in school, and thereby wind up as 'academic casualties'. These youngsters can be grouped into three general categories, including late developers and slow learners. In this chapter I will describe the unique characteristics of the third group.

The underachiever

The underachiever is a student who is unsuccessful in school *despite* his ability to do the work. He may have an IQ of 120 or more, yet do poorly at school. Underachievers are less understood (and more numerous) than either slow learners or late developers.

The apparent confusion about this group is related to the fact that *two* specific qualities are necessary to produce academic excellence, the second of which is often overlooked. First, *intellectual ability* must be there. But mental capacity is insufficient by itself. *Self-discipline* is also required. An able child may or may not have the self-control necessary to bear down day after day on something he considers painful and difficult.

Intelligence and self-discipline are frequently *not* correlated. A child often has one without the other. Occasionally, an untalented child will struggle to achieve above his expected level. This phenomenon is called overachievement. The opposite combination, known as underachievement, is much more common. It is typified by the child who has considerable intellectual potential but insists on wasting it.

It is apparent that underachievers are handled in a way that compounds their problem. This is because, as indicated in Chapter 7, we often fail to acknowledge that learning requires the hardest kind of effort. Examine for a moment what is required of a secondary school student in a daily homework assignment. He must understand what the teacher wants, including page numbers and other details. He must remember to bring home the right book. He must turn off the television set and ignore the phone in the evening. He must concentrate on the task long enough to do it correctly. He must take the finished product back to class the following day and hand it in. He must remember what he learned until the next test. Lastly, he must complete these homework assignments more than once or twice; they must be done repeatedly throughout the year.

This kind of performance requires more than intelligence. The fact that a child has a good vocabulary and can piece together various manipulative puzzles does not mean he can push himself week after week, year after year. Some children succeed through the primary school years, but give up later. In fact, it has been estimated that in the USA, 75 per cent of all students experience an academic slump sometime between the ages of twelve and fifteen. Despite this common occurrence, neither the school nor the home is usually prepared to deal with it.

The typical parent reacts in one of three ways to their underachieving child.

The first reaction is treating the problem as though it resulted from sheer stubbornness. Thus, parents may take away the bicycle for six months, ground the youngster until spring, or tear into his personhood and position in the family. Assuming the accuracy of my premise (that the behaviour results from an understandable, childish lack of self-control), this reaction will not make consistent bookwork any likelier. Under these conditions, school takes on the blue hue of threat, which hardly makes the youngster more diligent.

Parents who become angry about underachievement in their child might also find studying difficult if they were suddenly thrust back in school. Resistance to mental exercise is considered natural in a mature adult but in an immature child it is assumed to reflect stubbornness.

The second approach is to offer the child a long-range bribe: a new bicycle in a couple of years or a trip to a theme park next summer. These delayed offers are also ineffective for reasons outlined in a previous chapter. Postponed reinforcement is tantamount to no reinforcement.

The third parental reaction is to say, 'He's got to learn responsibility sometime! I can't always be there to help—so it's his problem.'

If parents seem unrealistic in handling the difficulty, some schools may not be any more helpful. Teachers and counsellors sometimes tell parents, 'Don't worry about it. Johnny will outgrow the problem.' That's the biggest falsehood of the year. Johnny usually doesn't outgrow the problem—gross underachievement in the primary years tends to be rather persistent. Furthermore, I've observed that most underachievers are lifelong 'messies'. They are often sloppy and disorganised in everything they do. It is a persistent trait that goes cross-grain to what is needed in the classroom.

Over the years I have dealt with more than 500 under-achievers and have concluded that there are only two functional solutions to this syndrome. The first is certainly no panacea: parents can become so involved in the schoolwork that the child has no choice but to do the job. This is possible only if the school takes the time to communicate assignments and progress to the parents, because the child certainly won't carry the message! Adolescents, particularly, will confound the communication between school and home as much as possible.

In one of the high schools where I served, for example, the students had a period of twenty minutes each day which was used for council meetings, announcements and related matters. Very little opportunity for studying occurred there, yet each day hundreds of parents were told that all the homework was finished during that session. The naive parents were led to believe that the period was a lengthy block of concentrated effort. Parents must know what goes on in school if they want to influence their child's academic responsibilities.

Also, the parents should provide *support* in areas where pure self-discipline is needed. The evening study period should be highly structured—routine hours and a minimum of interferences. The parent must know what was assigned and how the finished product should look. Ongoing research by the Center for the Study of the Family, Children, and Youth at Stanford University, USA, is finding that one method of helping the underachiever that results in a sustained improvement in schoolwork is parental involvement. When Mum and Dad offer regular encouragement, praise for a job well done, and meaningful assistance, grades tend to go up.[1]

I must hasten to say that this can be quite difficult. Intense parental involvement can rarely be sustained for more than a week or two, because many mums and dads don't have the required self-discipline themselves. There must be a way to supplement their effort, and I believe there is.

The underachiever often thrives under a system of immediate reinforcement, as described previously. If the child is not challenged by the rewards and motivators given at school, he'll need additional incentives. These positive reinforcements should be based on definite, reachable goals. Further, the payoff should be applied to small units of behaviour. Instead of rewarding the child for earning an 'A' in the English exam at the end of the year, he should be given five or ten pence for each maths problem accurately calculated.

'Bribery!' some readers will charge.

'Who cares?' is my reply, if it puts the child to work.

The use of immediate reinforcement serves the same function as a starter motor on a car. You can't drive very far with it, but it gets the engine going much easier than pushing. For the idealist who objects to using this extrinsic motivation, I would ask: 'What alternative do we have, other than to "let the child grow out of his problem"?'

Several examples may illustrate the specific application of reinforcement within the school setting. One of the most successful uses of this technique occurred with a classic underachiever named Billy, who, though eight, was kept back in the class for seven-year-olds. His motivation had been assassinated by early failures, and he did nothing in school. Furthermore, his younger sister was also in that class, having been promoted the same year Billy was held back. And wouldn't you know, she was an academic whizz while Billy was mired in intellectual despair.

After talking to his mother, we agreed upon a motivation system to be implemented at home. On the basis of our conference, Billy's mother quickly constructed the chart on page 188.

For each five minutes Billy spent working on his weekly spelling words with a parent, he got to colour in a bar on the chart. When all bars were coloured, he would receive a new bicycle seat. He also coloured a bar for each ten minutes spent working on arithmetic flash cards. Fifty bars would earn him a bowling trip with his father. Billy's mother considered reading to be his biggest problem. Thus, reading provided the pathway to a day at the amusement park. As the biggest prize, it naturally took longer to earn (one bar was coloured for each fifteen minutes of reading).

By staggering the reinforcement, one pleasant reward could be earned quickly, another soon after, and a grand prize waited at the end. Billy quickly caught the excitement of the game. He rushed home after school and went to work with his mother. Whereas she was previously unable to make him open a book, he suddenly wanted to 'study' throughout the evening. The reinforcement

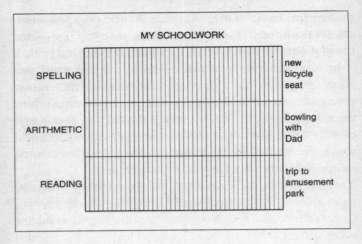

system worked so well that it had an unexpected consequence. Billy's mother called me the following week to complain about not being able to get her work done when Billy was at home!

After a while, a strange thing began to happen. Billy began to learn, though that was not his intent. He spelled all his words correctly on the weekly test for the first time, and enjoyed the feeling of success that followed. When the class was discussing arithmetic he knew the answers, and waved his hand for a chance to prove his knowledge. His reading improved noticeably, and his teacher moved him out of the slow reading group. Without meaning to do so, Billy discovered the joy of learning. The vicious cycle of failure had been broken.

It would be wrong to imply that all learning problems can be eliminated as easily and successfully as Billy's. Some underachievers are 'hard-core' and *nothing* will shake them loose. Yet reinforcement offers the best possibility for improvement. This system has been employed throughout the world, often with remarkable results.

In New York City, for example, it was used to help many delinquent youths who couldn't read. The young rebels, who would have laughed off a direct offer to teach them to read, had to be enticed via the back door. That's exactly what happened. Researchers told them, 'Look, we've got some machines that *might* be able to teach reading, but we need your help to determine if they work. There's money involved: we'll actually pay you for each right answer.' The amount of money was decent for the summer programme, and most of the adolescents who accepted the offer learned to read. This, in turn, helped steer them off the street and into the classroom, thereby opening new academic challenges to them.

A similar system was applied in Alabama prisons, whereby inmates could earn money by learning new skills and completing instructional courses. The future will bring even wider application of these principles to difficult behavioural problems, including the one of academic underachievement.

Children and adolescents, like people of all ages, want to be responsible. They want to feel the self-respect and dignity of doing what is right. The ones who fail in school are often the most miserable, but they lack the self-discipline to overcome their own inertia.

Summary

In these past two chapters, I have described three great barriers to discipline in the classroom. Of course there are additional problems which I have not presented in detail. Anything that worries or troubles a child can result in school failure. For example, deep feelings of inadequacy and inferiority can prevent academic concentration. The child who must cope with such emotions has little time for less important matters. Adults who have tried to work or think while awaiting a threatening medical report, such as a lab test for cancer, may understand this mechanism of mental interference.

Parents and teachers must never underestimate the threats a child associates with school. Regardless of whether or not he verbalises his fears, he is often aware of many 'dangers' which lurk just inside the school gate. That is, other students might laugh at him. He may be ridiculed or criticised by teachers. He could be rejected by members of the opposite sex. He may fail despite his best efforts. These and similar fears can permeate the entire world of a bewildered young student, causing him to act in ways which appear lazy. Thus, the solution to school failure often requires dealing with problems which seem unrelated to classroom work.

One further thought strikes me as very important at this point. We have discussed three categories of children, those who are late developers, slow learners, or under-achievers. But how can a parent or teacher know if a child has one of these problems or some other intellectual deficit? The answer in a particular case can only be deter-mined from a complete educational assessment con-ducted by a person trained and qualified to evaluate children. In each of the three categories I have described, a test of intelligence (IQ) is necessary to identify a child's problem. How can we know the underachiever is not a slow learner unless we measure basic intellectual skills? How can we separate the late developer from a child with a severe learning deficit without assessing fundamental abilities? The IQ test is an extremely valuable tool in this differentiation.

Unfortunately, IQ testing has all but disappeared in many schools, and is not routinely carried out in many countries, including Britain. Because these instruments (such as the WISC-R or Stanford Binet) were perceived to be unfair to minorities, their use has come under increasing criticism in recent years. Thus, it is no longer 'politically correct' to use them. As a result, parents who desperately need the information previously available from testing in state school settings now have to seek out a psychologist or counsellor in private practice who can conduct the evaluation. Those who lack the funds to obtain this expensive assistance, including many minorities, are deprived of the help their children need. I regret the political situation that prevents school districts from evaluating their students with the best tests available.

But what about minorities? Are standardised IQ tests unfair to immigrant communities? I do not think so. It is true that minorities sometimes do more poorly on these tests because their cultures do not prepare them for that kind of exam. But read carefully now: the same cultural factors that affect the test results also affect school performance. Performance on test questions is correlated with classroom work. If we seek a test that does not reflect the impact of an inner-city culture, then it will be useless because it will no longer *predict* classroom performance.

Let me say it once more. The purpose of testing is to estimate how well a given child is likely to do in an academic setting. To create an instrument that will not reflect the handicap his culture will place on him, when that culture will definitely handicap him in the classroom, is to play games with 'political correctness'.

Q *It is my understanding that we forget 80 per cent of everything we learn in three months' time and a higher percentage is forgotten as time passes. Why, then, should we put children through the agony of learning? Why is mental exercise needed if the effort is so inefficient?*

A Your question reflects the viewpoint of the old progressive education theorists. They wanted the school curriculum to be nothing more than 'life adjustment'. They placed a low priority on intellectual discipline for the reasons you mentioned. Even some college lecturers have adopted this 'no content' philosophy, as I have mentioned elsewhere. They reason that the material we learn today may be obsolete tomorrow, so why learn it? I strongly disagree with this approach to education. There are at least five reasons why learning is important, even if we forget much of what we're taught:

1. As indicated earlier, teaching self-discipline is a very important component of the academic experience. Good students learn to sit for long hours, follow directions, complete assignments, and use their mental faculties. Accordingly, homework is relatively unimportant as an educational tool; it *is* a valuable instrument of discipline. Since adult life often requires self-sacrifice, sweat, and devotion to causes, school should help shape a child's capacity to handle this future responsibility. Certainly, play is important in a child's life, too.

Youngsters should not work all the time. The home and school should provide a healthy balance between discipline and play.

2. Learning is important because we are *changed* by what we learn, even if the facts are later forgotten. No college graduate could remember everything he has learned, yet he is a very different person for having gone to college. Learning changes values, attitudes and concepts which don't fade in time.

3. Even if the learned material cannot be recalled, the individual knows the facts exist and where to find them. If we asked a complicated question of an uneducated man, he would probably give a definite, unqualified response. The same question would probably be answered more cautiously by a person with an advanced degree. The latter individual would say, 'Well, there are several ways to look at it . . .' He knows the matter is more complex than it appears, even if he doesn't have the complete answer.

4. We don't forget 100 per cent of what we learn. The most important facts lodge in our permanent memory for future use. The human brain is capable of storing 2,000 million bits of data in a lifetime; education is the process of filling that memory bank with useful information.

5. Old learning makes new learning easier. Each mental exercise gives us more associative cues with which to link future ideas and concepts.

I wish there were an easier, more efficient process for shaping human minds than the slow, painful experience of education. But I'm afraid we must depend on this old-fashioned approach until a 'learning pill' is developed.

Q *Some educators have said we should eliminate reports and academic marks. Do you think this is a good idea?*

A No, academic marks are valuable for students eight years old and over. They reinforce and reward the child who has achieved in school and nudge the youngster who hasn't. It is important, though, that marks be used properly. They have the power to create or destroy motivation.

Through the primary-school years and in required courses at secondary school, a child's exam results should be based on what he does with what he has. In other words, I think we should grade according to ability. A slow child should be able to succeed in school just as certainly as a gifted youngster. If he struggles and sweats to achieve, he should somehow be rewarded—even if his work falls short of an absolute standard. By the same token, gifted children should not be given 'As' just because they are smart enough to excel without working.

The primary purpose in grading should be to reward academic effort. Those who disagree should consider the alternative reflected in the following illustration: Joe is less than brilliant and knows it. At the age of seven he gave up trying to do well in school. However, when he reached secondary school he was taught by a man who challenged him to do his best. He worked very hard to please this teacher, despite his problems with reading, writing and arithmetic.

At the end of the term, Joe was still hard at work, although his writing had improved little and he was struggling with a junior level reader. What was his teacher to do with Joe's report card? If he marked the youngster in relation to his peers, he would have to fail him. If he failed him, Joe would never work again.

Since Joe had done his best, should he receive the same result he got last year when he sat with unfocused eyes day after day? I think not. Joe should be praised for his diligence in the most obvious manner and given at least average marks on his report. The teacher should quietly inform his parents of the bigger picture, and enlist their support in encouraging Joe's continued effort.

Any other system of marking will result in discouragement to children of lesser ability. Even sharper students usually work better when they must stretch for excellence.

One exception to the 'grade on ability' policy should be implemented: college preparation courses in secondary school must be measured on an absolute standard. An 'A' in chemistry or mathematics is accepted by college admission boards as a symbol of excellence, and schoolteachers must preserve that meaning. But then, Joe and his friends need not take those difficult courses.

To repeat, marks can be the teacher's most important motivational tool—provided they are used correctly. Therefore, the recommendation that schools eliminate grading is a move away from discipline in the classroom.

Q *My child has what has been called an attention deficit disorder (ADD) that makes it hard for him to do well in school. I understand his difficulty. But he fails most of his exams, and I know that will limit his opportunities in life. What should be the attitude of a parent towards a child who fails year after year?*

A Obviously, tutorial assistance and special instruction should be provided, if possible. Beyond that, however, I would strongly suggest that academic achievement be de-emphasised at home for the youngster who has a demonstrated learning difficulty.

Requiring a child with ADD or dyslexia (a specific reading disability) to compete academically is like forcing a child with cerebral palsy to run the 100 metres. Imagine a mother and father standing disapprovingly at the end of the track, berating their handicapped child as he hobbles across the finish line in last place.

'Why don't you run faster, son?' his mother asks with obvious displeasure.

'I don't think you really care whether you win or lose,' says his embarrassed father.

How can this lad explain that his legs will not carry him as fast as those of his peers? All he knows is that the other sprinters run past him to the cheering of the crowd. But who would expect a disabled child to win a race against healthy peers? No one, simply because his handicap is obvious. Everyone can see it.

Unfortunately, the child with a learning difficulty is not so well understood. His academic failure is more difficult to understand and may be attributed to laziness, mischievousness, or deliberate defiance. Consequently, he experiences pressures to do the impossible. And one of the most serious threats to emotional health occurs when a child faces demands that he cannot satisfy.

Let me restate the preceding viewpoint in its most concise terms. I believe in academic excellence. I want to maximise every ounce of intellectual potential which a child possesses. I don't believe in letting him behave irresponsibly simply because he doesn't choose to work. Without question, there is a lasting benefit to be derived from educational discipline.

On the other hand, some things in life are more important than academic excellence, and self-esteem is one of them. A child can survive, if he must, without knowing a noun from a verb. But if he doesn't have some measure of self-confidence and personal respect, he won't have a chance in life.

I want to assert my conviction that the child who is unequipped to prosper in the traditional setting is not inferior to his peers. He possesses the same degree of human worth and dignity as the intellectual young superstar. It is a foolish cultural distortion that causes us to evaluate the worth of children according to the abilities and physical features they may (or may not) possess.

Every child is of equal worth in the sight of God, and that is good enough for me. Thus, if my little boy or girl can't be successful in one environment, we'll just look for another. Any loving parent would do the same.[2]

10

Discipline in Morality

My friend and colleague, attorney Gary Bauer, served for eight years in the Reagan administration, ultimately being appointed Senior Domestic Policy Advisor to the president. During his latter years in the White House, Bauer also headed an historic commission on the family that revealed surprising findings about America's adolescents.

After two years of investigation, Bauer's commission learned that Americans in every age category were better off at the time of the study than they had been ten years earlier. Both adults and younger children were found to be more healthy, better fed and better educated than before. More tax money was being spent on children and more programmes and bureaucrats were in place to address their needs. There was, however, a striking exception to this conclusion.

Teenagers were found to be considerably *worse* off than in the previous decade. Their many problems could not be blamed on government, on educators or on the medical community. Rather, Bauer and his co-workers found that young people were busily killing *themselves* at an alarming rate. It is shocking to see just how hostile the world of the young has become and how poorly they are coping with their difficulties.

Suppose the parents of yesterday could visit our time to observe the conditions that prevail among our children. They would be appalled by the problems which have become widespread (and are spreading wider) in our homes, schools and neighbourhoods.

Gang violence and one-to-one crime among the young is an indescribable shame. Wandering droves of children and teenagers are knifing and bludgeoning each other at an unprecedented rate. It is not unusual in the large cities for ten or fifteen young people to die in a single violent weekend, with shootings increasingly common in America. Emergency units of virtually every inner city hospital are taxed to the limit trying to deal with the casualties of gang warfare now being waged. They call it 'battlefield medicine'. The killings are so common that many don't even get reported in the news. Only when the body count reaches record proportions do people seem alarmed by what is happening. Who would have believed in 1970 when *Dare to Discipline* was first written that this would have occurred?

Isaac Fulwood, Chief of Police in Washington, DC, blamed the city's 'love of drugs', when the homicide rate there set another record for the third consecutive year.[1] He could have just as easily pointed his finger at City Hall. At that same time, Mayor Marion Barry was making headlines around the country (and a mockery of law enforcement) for his conviction of cocaine possession.

'The United States is breeding a lost generation of

children,' proclaimed one authority, citing teenage violence statistics compiled by the US Justice Department.
These figures showed that since 1983, robberies committed by juveniles under eighteen have increased five times,
murders have tripled, and rapes have doubled. The
leading killer of black males aged fifteen to twenty-four is
now homicide; only car accidents kill more white youths.[2]

'During every one hundred hours on our streets we lose
more young men than were killed in one hundred hours
of ground war in the Persian Gulf,' lamented Dr Louis
Sullivan, secretary of the Department of Health and
Human Services during the Bush administration. 'Where
are the yellow ribbons of hope and remembrance for our
youth dying in the streets?'[3]

Wherever one chooses to look within adolescent
society, trouble is evident. A root cause for much of the
unrest, of course, is the continued prevalence of alcohol
and substance abuse by the young. A recent Gallup
Report indicated that before leaving school a staggering
percentage of teenagers are hooked on mind-altering
drugs of some type. Eighty-five per cent experiment with
alcohol. Fifty-seven per cent try an illicit drug, and 35 per
cent get drunk at least once a month.[4] And lest those of
us with Christian homes get complacent, there is not
much difference between churched and unchurched families in the evidence of teenage substance abuse.[5]

There is an ache deep within my spirit over what we
have allowed to happen to our kids. What is it going to
take to alarm the mass of humanity that sits on the side-
lines watching our kids struggle for survival? It is time for
every God-fearing adult to get on our faces in repentance
before the Almighty. *We* have permitted this mess to

occur! *We* allowed immoral television and movie producers to make their fortunes by exploiting our kids. *We* allowed their filth and their horribly violent productions to come into our homes via cable, video, CDs, and network trash. *We* stood by passively while 'sex education' taught our teenagers to be sexually promiscuous. *We* allowed them to invade our schools and promote an alien value system that contradicted everything we believed and loved. *We* granted profit-motivated abortionists unsupervised and unreported access to our minor daughters, while we were thinking about something else. *We,* as parents, are guilty of abandoning our children to those who would use them for their own purposes. Where in God's name have we been? How bad does it have to get before we say, 'Enough is enough!'?

At the core of these individual tragedies is a moral catastrophe that has rocked our families to their foundation. We have forgotten God and disregarded his holy ordinances. But it is our children who have suffered and will continue to pay for our lack of stewardship and diligence.

Of all the dimensions wherein we have mishandled this younger generation, none is more disgraceful than the sexual immorality that has permeated the world in which they live. There is no more effective way to destroy the institution of the family than to undermine the sexual exclusivity on which it is based. Yet that has been accomplished, deliberately and thoughtfully, by those who despised the Christian system of values. Today's 'safe-sex' advocates are advancing that campaign with devastating effectiveness.

In 1991, the humanistic organisation known as the Sex Information and Education Council of the United States

(SIECUS) assembled a task force of twenty educators, social workers and health personnel who were asked to draw up a comprehensive sex education programme for children and young people. They prepared a forty-page report for local officials preparing sex education curricula, entitled *Guidelines for Comprehensive Sexuality Education*. The individual members of the task force are among the foremost moulders of opinion and sexual behaviour among the young. Take a look at what they advocate for those in their teen years.

—People do not choose their sexual orientation.
—The traditional gender roles about sexuality in our society are becoming more flexible.
—The telephone number of the gay and lesbian switchboard is _____.
—There does not have to be prescribed gender roles for dating partners.
—Masturbation either alone or with a partner is one way a person can enjoy and express their [sic] sexuality without risking pregnancy or an STD/HIV.
—Some people use erotic photographs, movies or literature to enhance their sexual fantasies when alone or with a partner.
—The right of a woman to have an abortion is guaranteed by the Supreme Court, although there are restrictions in some states.
—Gender role stereotypes can lead to such problems as low aspirations, low paying jobs, date rape, and stress-related illnesses.
—There is no evidence that erotic images in the arts cause inappropriate sexual behaviour.

—Teenagers can get confidential testing and treatment for STD/HIV without parental consent.

—Many religions today acknowledge that human beings were created to be sexual beings, and that their sexuality is good.[6]

The task force that prepared these guidelines clearly has an agenda, including the promotion of homosexuality, abortion on demand, sexual relations among unmarried people, unrestricted access to pornography by the young, and so on. How about it, parents? Is this what you want taught to *your* teenagers? I don't believe the majority of today's mothers and fathers agree with these objectives, but most don't care enough to oppose it, apparently.

Well, the organisation I represent *is* concerned enough to speak out, as is our partner organisation in the UK, Care for the Family. We will do everything we can to save this generation of kids, who now face the threat of death from the dreaded HIV. We are passive no longer.

In 1992, Focus on the Family placed a full-page ad in *USA Today* to explain the *health* risks associated with the myth of safe sex. Its contents are so vital that I am including the entire statement, along with appropriate references, on the pages that follow. Please note as you read that even if morality were of no consequence, the sex liberators are creating enormous medical problems for us. Sooner or later, the epidemic of sexually transmitted diseases will expose the lies our kids have been told.

In Defence of a Little Virginity
A message from Focus on the Family

The federal government has spent almost $3 billion of our taxes since 1970 to promote contraceptives and safe sex among our teenagers. Isn't it time we asked, What have we got for our money? These are the facts:

—The federal Centers for Disease Control estimate that there are now one million cases of HIV infection nationwide.[7]

—1 in 100 students coming to the University of Texas health center now carries the deadly virus.[8]

—The rate of heterosexual HIV transmission has increased 44 per cent since September 1989.[9]

—Sexually transmitted diseases (STDs) infect 3 million teenagers annually.[10]

—63 per cent of all STD cases occur among persons less than twenty-five years of age.[11]

—1 million new cases of pelvic inflammatory disease occur annually.[12]

—1.3 million new cases of gonorrhea occur annually;[13] strains of gonorrhea have developed that are resistant to penicillin.

—Syphilis is at a forty-year high, with 134,000 new infections per year.[14]

—500,000 new cases of herpes occur annually;[15] it is estimated that 16.4 per cent of the U.S. population ages fifteen to seventy-four is infected, totalling more than 25 million Americans—among certain groups, the infection rate is as high as 60 per cent.[16]

—4 million cases of chlamydia occur annually;[17] 10 to 30 per cent of fifteen- to nineteen-year-olds are infected.[18]

—There are now 24 million cases of human papilloma virus (HPV), with a higher prevalence among teens.[19]

To date, over twenty different and dangerous sexually transmitted diseases are rampant among the young. Add to that the problems associated with promiscuous behavior: infertility, abortions and infected newborns. The cost of this epidemic is staggering, both in human suffering and in expense to society; yet epidemiologists tell us we've only seen the beginning.

Incredibly, the safe-sex gurus and condom promoters who got us into this mess are still determining our policy regarding adolescent sexuality. Their ideas have failed, and it is time to rethink their bankrupt policies.

How long has it been since you've heard anyone tell teenagers why it is to their advantage to remain virgins until married? The facts are being withheld from them, with tragic consequences. Unless we come to terms with the sickness that stalks a generation of Americans, teen promiscuity will continue, and millions of kids . . . thinking they are protected . . . will suffer for the rest of their lives. Many will die of AIDS.

There is only one safe way to remain healthy in the midst of a sexual revolution. It is to abstain from intercourse until marriage, and then wed and be faithful to an uninfected partner. It is a concept that was widely endorsed in society until the 1960s. Since then, a better idea has come along . . . one that now threatens the entire human family.

Inevitable questions are raised whenever abstinence is proposed. It's time we gave some clear answers:

Why, apart from moral considerations, do you think teenagers should be taught to abstain from sex until marriage?

No other approach to the epidemic of sexually transmitted diseases will work. The so-called safe-sex solution is a disaster in the making. Condoms can fail at least 15.7 per cent of the time annually in preventing pregnancy.[20] They fail 36.3 per cent of the time annually in preventing pregnancy among young, unmarried minority women.[21] In a study of homosexual men, the *British Medical Journal* reported the failure rate due to slippage and breakage to be 26 per cent.[22] Given these findings, it is obvious why we have a word for people who rely on condoms as a means of birth control. We call them . . . parents.

Remembering that a woman can conceive only one or two days per month, we can only guess how high the failure rate for condoms must be in preventing disease, which can be transmitted 365 days per year! If the devices are not used properly, or if they slip just once, viruses and bacteria are exchanged and the disease process begins. One mistake after five hundred protected episodes is all it takes to contract a sexually transmitted disease. The damage is done in a single moment when rational thought is overridden by passion.

Those who would depend on so insecure a method must use it properly on every occasion, and even then a high failure rate is brought about by factors beyond their control. The young victim who is told by his elders that this little latex device is safe may not know he is risking lifelong pain and even death for so brief a window of pleasure. What a burden to place on an immature mind and body!

Then we must recognize that there are other differences between pregnancy prevention and disease prevention. HIV is one twenty-fifth the width of sperm,[23] and can pass easily through even the smallest gaps in condoms. Researchers studying surgical gloves made out of latex, the same material in condoms, found channels of 5 microns that penetrated the entire thickness of the glove.[24] HIV measures 0.1 microns.[25] Given these findings, what rational, informed person would trust his or her very life to such flimsy armor?

This surely explains why not one of eight hundred sexologists at a conference a few years ago raised a hand when asked if they would trust a thin rubber sheath to protect them during intercourse with a known HIV-infected person.[26] Who could blame them? They're not crazy, after all. And yet they're perfectly willing to tell our kids that safe sex is within reach and that they can sleep around with impunity.

There is only one way to protect ourselves from the deadly diseases that lie in wait. It is abstinence before marriage, then marriage and mutual fidelity for life to an uninfected partner. Anything less is potentially suicidal.

That position is simply NOT realistic today. It's an unworkable solution: Kids will NOT implement it.

Some will. Some won't. It's still the only answer. But let's talk about an unworkable solution of the first order. Since 1970, the federal government has spent nearly $3 billion to promote contraception and safe sex. This year alone, 450 million of your tax dollars will go down that drain![27] (Compared with less than $8 million for abstinence programs, which Sen. Teddy Kennedy and company have sought repeatedly to eliminate altogether.) Isn't it time we ask what we've gotten for our money? After twenty-two years and nearly $3 billion, some 58 per cent of teenage girls under eighteen still did not use contraception during their first intercourse.[28] Furthermore, teenagers tend to keep having unprotected intercourse for a full year, on average, before starting any kind of contraception.[29] That is the success ratio of the experts who call abstinence unrealistic and unworkable.

Even if we spent another $50 billion to promote condom usage, most teenagers would still not use them consistently and properly. The nature of human beings and the passion of the act simply do not lend themselves to a disciplined response in young romantics.

But if you knew a teenager was going to have intercourse, wouldn't you teach him or her about proper condom usage?

No, because that approach has an unintended consequence. The process of recommending condom usage to teenagers inevitably conveys five dangerous ideas: (1) that safe sex is achievable; (2) that everybody is doing it; (3) that responsible adults expect them to do it; (4) that it's a good thing; and (5) that their peers know they know these things, breeding promiscuity. Those are very destructive messages to give our kids.

Furthermore, Planned Parenthood's own data show that the number one reason teenagers engage in intercourse is peer pressure![30] Therefore, anything we do to imply that everybody is doing it results in more . . . not fewer . . . people who give the game a try. Condom distribution programs do not reduce the number of kids exposed to disease . . . they radically increase it!

Want proof of that fact? Since the federal government began its major contraception program in 1970, unwed pregnancies have increased 87 per cent among fifteen- to nineteen-year-olds.[31] Likewise, abortions among teens rose 67 per cent;[32] unwed births went up 61 per cent.[33] And venereal disease has infected a generation of young people. Nice job, sex counselors. Good thinking, senators and congressmen. Nice nap, America.

Having made a blunder that now threatens the human family, one would think the designers would be backtracking and apologizing for their miscalculations. Instead, they continue to lobby Congress and corporate America for more money. Given the misinformation extant on this subject, they'll probably get it.

But if you were a parent and knew that your son or daughter was having sex, wouldn't you rather he or she used a condom?

How much risk is acceptable when you're talking about your teenager's life? One study of married couples in which one partner was infected with HIV found that 17 per cent of the partners using condoms for protection still caught the virus within a year and a half.[34] Telling our teens to reduce their risk to one in six (17 per cent) is not much better than advocating Russian roulette. Both are fatal, eventually. The difference is that with a gun, death is quicker. Suppose your son or daughter were joining an eighteen-month skydiving club of six members. If you knew that one of their parachutes would definitely fail, would you recommend that they simply buckle the chutes tighter? Certainly not. You would say, 'Please don't jump! Your life is at stake!' How could a loving parent do less?

Kids won't listen to the abstinence message. You're just wasting your breath to try to sell them a notion like that.

It is a popular myth that teenagers are incapable of understanding that it is in their best interest to save themselves until marriage. Almost 65 per cent of all high school females under eighteen are virgins.[35]

A few years ago in Lexington, Ky., a youth event was held that featured no sports contest, no rock groups—just an ex-convict named Harold Morris talking about abstinence, among other subjects. The coliseum seated 15,000 people, but 26,000 teenagers showed up! Eventually more than 2,000 stood outside the packed auditorium and listened over a hastily prepared public address system. Who says kids won't listen to this time-honored message?

Even teens who have been sexually active can choose to stop. This is often called secondary virginity, a good concept that conveys the idea that kids can start over. One young girl recently wrote Ann Landers to say she wished she had kept her virginity, signing the letter, 'Sorry I didn't and wish I could take it back.' As responsible adults we need to tell her that even though she can't go back, she can go forward. She can regain her self-respect and protect her health, because it's never too late to start saying no to premarital sex.

Even though the safe-sex advocates predominate in educational circles, are there no positive examples of abstinence-based programs for kids?

Thankfully, some excellent programs have been developed. Spokane-based Teen-Aid and Chicago's Southwest Parents Committee are good examples. So are Next Generation in Maryland, Choices in California, and Respect Inc. in Illinois. Other curricula such as Facing Reality; Sex Respect; Me, My World, My Future; Reasonable Reasons to Wait; Sex, Love & Choices; and F.A.C.T.S. etc. are all abstinence-themed programs to help kids make good sexual decisions.

A good curriculum for inner-city youth is Elayne Bennett's Best Friends program. This successful mentoring project helps adolescents in Washington, D.C. graduate from high school and remain abstinent. In five years, not one female has become pregnant while in the Best Friends program!

Establishing and nurturing abstinence ideas with kids, however, can be like spitting into the wind. Not because they won't listen, because most will. But pro-abstinence messages are drowned out in a sea of toxic teen-sex-is-inevitable-use-a-condom propaganda from safe-sex professionals. You place major responsibility on those who have told adolescents that sexual expression is their right as long as they do it properly. Who else has contributed to the epidemic?

The entertainment industry must certainly share the blame, including television producers. It is interesting in this context that all four networks and the cable television entities are wringing their hands about this terrible epidemic of AIDS. They profess to be very concerned about those who are infected with sexually transmitted diseases, and perhaps they are sincere. However, TV executives and movie moguls have contributed mightily to the existence of this plague. For decades, they have depicted teens and young adults climbing in and out of each other's beds like so many sexual robots. Only the nerds were shown to be chaste, and they were too stupid or ugly to find partners.

Of course, the beautiful young actors in those steamy

dramas never faced any consequences for their sexual indulgence. No one ever came down with herpes, or syphilis, or chlamydia, or pelvic inflammatory disease, or infertility, or AIDS, or genital warts, or cervical cancer. No patients were ever told by a physician that there was no cure for their disease or that they would have to deal with the pain for the rest of their lives. No one ever heard that genital cancers associated with the human papilloma virus (HPV) kill more women than AIDS,[36] or that strains of gonorrhea are now resistant to penicillin.[37]

No, there was no downside. It all looked like so much fun. But what a price we are paying now for the lies we have been told.

The government has also contributed to this crisis and continues to exacerbate the problem. For example, a current brochure from the federal Centers for Disease Control and the city of New York is entitled 'Teens Have the Right' and is apparently intended to free adolescents from adult authority. Inside are the six declarations that make up a Teenagers Bill of Rights, as follows:

—I have the right to think for myself.
—I have the right to decide to have sex and who[m] to have it with.
—I have the right to use protection when I have sex.
—I have the right to buy and use condoms.
—I have the right to express myself.
—I have the right to ask for help if I need it.

Under this final item (the right to ask for help) is a list of organizations and phone numbers that readers are encouraged to call. The philosophy that governs several of the organizations reflects the homosexual agenda, which includes a recruitment of the young and vigorous promotion of a teens right to sexual expression.

Your tax dollars at work!

Surely there are other Americans who recognize the danger now threatening a generation of our best and brightest. It is time to speak up for an old-fashioned value called virginity. Now, more than ever, virtue is a necessity.

The response to this advertisement and to our continued distribution of its message was overwhelming. More than 50,000 letters came to our offices from enthusiastic parents, teachers, health workers and church leaders who applauded our efforts. Many have felt exactly as we do, but perceived themselves to be powerless against the media and the government-sponsored purveyors of propaganda. But the time has come for action. It's time to tell the Government to stop funding suicidal safe-sex programmes . . . or else. It's time to teach old fashioned principles of morality to our children . . . not just because it's the only safe approach, but because it's *right*. It's in harmony with the prescription of him who said:

> Woe to those who call evil good and good evil, who put darkness for light and light for darkness, who put bitter for sweet and sweet for bitter . . . Therefore, as tongues of fire lick up straw and as dry grass sinks down in the flames, so their roots will decay and their flowers blow away like dust; for they have rejected the law of the Lord Almighty and spurned the word of the Holy One of Israel (Is 5:20, 24, NIV).

A few words about sex education

I have devoted the remainder of this chapter to parents and teachers who believe in moral decency and want to instil responsible sexual attitudes in their children. Their task is not an easy one. The sexual urge is stronger during adolescence than in any other period of life, and there is no way to guarantee that an independent teenager will choose to control it. It is impossible to shield these youth from the permissive attitudes which are prevalent today. Television brings every aspect of sexual gratification into the sanctuary of one's living room, and the details of immorality and perversion are readily available in the cinema or from the local video store. Obviously, solitary confinement for a child is not the answer.

Furthermore, there is a danger that parents will make one mistake in their efforts to avoid another. While attempting to teach discipline in matters of morality, they must be careful not to inculcate unhealthy attitudes that will interfere with sexual fulfilment in future marital relations. Those who would teach this subject have the difficult responsibility of saying 'sex can be wonderful' and 'sex can be dangerous' in the same breath, which takes some doing.

How then can conscientious adults instil self-control in their children without generating deep emotional hang-ups or negative attitudes? Discussed below are the aspects of sex education which are critical to the achievement of this delicate task.

Who should teach the child about sex?

The task of forming healthy sexual attitudes and understanding in children requires considerable skill and tact, and parents are often keenly aware of their lack of preparation to do the job. However, for those parents who *are* able to handle the instructional process correctly, the responsibility should be retained in the home. There is a growing trend for all aspects of education to be taken from the hands of parents (or the role is deliberately forfeited by them). This is a mistake.

Particularly in the matter of sex education, the best approach is one that begins in early childhood and extends through the years, according to a policy of openness, frankness and honesty. Only parents can provide this lifetime training.

The child's need for information and guidance is rarely met in one massive conversation by dry-mouthed, sweaty-palmed parents as their child approaches adolescence. Nor is a concentrated formal educational course outside the home the best alternative. The ideal approach is a gradual enlightenment that begins during the third or fourth year of life and culminates shortly before puberty.

Despite the desirability of sex education being handled by highly skilled parents, one must admit this is an unrealistic objective in many homes (perhaps the majority of them). Parents are often too sexually inhibited to present the subject with poise, or they may lack the necessary technical knowledge of the human body. For such families which cannot, or will not, teach their children the details of human reproduction, assistance must be sought from outside the home.

It is my strong conviction that churches believing in abstinence before marriage and in lifelong marital fidelity should step in and offer their help to families sharing that commitment. Where else will mums and dads find proponents of traditional morality in this permissive day? There is no other agency or institution likely to represent the theology of the church better than representatives of the church itself. It is puzzling to me why so few have accepted this challenge, given the attack on biblical concepts of morality today.

A few parents who have their children in Christian schools are able to get the help they need with sex education. Even there, however, the subject is often ignored or handled inadequately. What has developed, quite obviously, is an informational vacuum that sets the stage for far-reaching programmes in the state schools.

One of the problems with sex education as it is currently taught in state schools is that it breaks down the natural barriers between the sexes and makes familiarity and casual sexual experimentation much more likely to occur. It also strips kids—especially girls—of their modesty to have every detail of anatomy, physiology and condom usage made explicit in co-ed situations. Then, the following Friday night when the kids are on a date and attend a sexually explicit movie or watch a hot TV programme showing teenagers in bed with one another, it is just a tiny step to intercourse—whereas a hundred years ago it was an enormous decision to give up one's virginity.

For those mums and dads whose children are in state schools today, it is imperative that they investigate what is being taught in the name of sex education. You should examine curricular materials and textbooks. You can and must talk to the teachers and head about what they hope to communicate and you can withdraw your child from the school's sex education classes if necessary. Look carefully for the hidden agenda, such as pro-homosexual and lesbian behaviour, the safe-sex distortion, the belief that premarital intercourse is a 'right', and any suggestion that pits teenagers against their parents. Find out if a pro-abortion stance is taken, and if family planning organisations are invited into the classroom.

If these elements are there, I strongly suggest that you keep your children out of the classes. What better way is there to undermine the value system we have taught than to invest authority and leadership in a teacher who ridicules and undermines it? Not only would I not allow my youngster to participate in such a programme, but I would help organise parent groups to institute an abstinence-based curriculum in the school. And if that didn't work, I'd begin campaigning for new school governors. I might even campaign for that office myself.

Why is there so much resistance to abstinence-based programmes?

Well, some educators honestly believe that 'kids will be kids', so we should show them how to play the game right. I don't agree with them, but I can respect their honest difference of opinion. There are others, however, who are in the business of promoting promiscuity and abortion, who I believe have other motives. For them, something else is going on. The subject is not merely an intellectual debate about children and what is their best interest. No, the topic is highly inflammatory. They become incensed when the word *abstinence* is even mentioned. Have you ever wondered why?

I served on Secretary Otis Bowen's Teen Pregnancy Prevention Panel during the Reagan era. I accepted that responsibility because I thought our purpose was to prevent teenage pregnancies. During our first meeting in Washington, DC, however, I learned that fifteen of the eighteen panel members had other ideas. They were all 'safe-sex' gurus, who wanted to spend millions of federal dollars distributing condoms and immoral advice to the nation's teenagers. I can't describe how emotional they were about this objective. In time, I began to understand a little more of the motivation propelling the community that makes a living from teenage sexual irresponsibility.

I described them this way in the book I co-authored with Gary Bauer, entitled *Children at Risk*:

Let's deal with the obvious question head on: Why do bureaucrats and researchers and Planned Parenthood types fight so hard to preserve adolescent promiscuity? Why do they balk at the thought of intercourse occurring only in the context of marriage? Why have they completely *removed* the door marked 'Premarital Sex' for a generation of vulnerable teenagers?

Their motivation is not difficult to understand. Multiplied millions of dollars are generated each year in direct response to teenage sexual irresponsibility. Kids jumping into bed with each other is supporting entire industries of grateful adults. The abortion business alone brings in an estimated $600 million annually. Do you really believe the physicians, nurses, medical suppliers and bureaucrats who owe their livelihood to the killing of unborn babies would prefer that adolescents abstain until marriage?!

How about condom manufacturers or the producers of spermicide, 'the pill', IUDs, or diaphragms? Would they want their business decimated by a sweeping wave of morality among the young? I doubt it. Then there are the producers of antibiotics and other drugs for use in treating sexually transmitted diseases. They have a financial stake in continued promiscuity as well.

At the top of the list of those who profit from adolescent

irresponsibility, however, are those who are purportedly working to fight it! Planned Parenthood and similar organizations would simply fade away if they were ever fully successful in eliminating teen pregnancies. They currently receive an estimated $106 million in federal subsidies to carry out their mission, plus approximately $200 million in contributions from private sources. Do you *really* believe they want to kill the goose that lays those golden eggs?

Imagine how many jobs would be lost if kids quit playing musical beds with one another! This is why professionals who advise young people about sex are so emotional about the word *abstinence*. If that idea ever caught on, who would need the services of Planned Parenthood and their ilk? It's a matter of self-preservation.

To fully comprehend the danger posed by Planned Parenthood and related organizations, it is important to examine their philosophy and intent. What is their program? What do their leaders want? What would they do if given free rein? As I understand their agenda, it can be summarized in the following four-point plan:

1. *Provide 'value free' guidance on sexuality to teenagers.* Heaven forbid any preference for morality or sexual responsibility being expressed.

2. *Provide unlimited quantities of contraceptives to adolescents,* dispensed aggressively from clinics located on junior and senior high campuses. In so doing, a powerful statement is made to teenagers about adult approval of premarital sexual activity.

3. *Keep parents out of the picture by every means possible.* Staff members of Planned Parenthood can then assume the parental role and communicate libertarian philosophy to teens.

4. *Provide unlimited access to free abortions for young women who become pregnant;* again, without parental involvement or permission.

Incredibly, the American and Canadian public seem to 'buy' this outrageous plan, which would have brought a storm of protest from yesterday's parents. Imagine how your father or grandfather would have reacted if a school official had secretly given contraceptives to you or arranged a quiet abortion when you were a teenager. The entire community would have been incensed. Someone may well have been shot! Yet today's parents have tolerated this intrusion without so much as a peep of protest. Why? What has happened to that spirit of protection for our families—that fierce independence that bonded us together against the outside world? I wish I knew.[38]

When to say what

Let me offer some counsel now, to mothers and fathers who want to handle the instruction of their own children and are looking for a few helpful 'how-tos'. I take my hat off to them. Even in this enlightened day, the subject of sex is charged with emotion. There are few thoughts which disturb Mum and Dad's tranquillity more than the vision of answering all of their children's probing questions—particularly the ones which become uncomfortably personal.

This tension was apparent in the mother of nine-year-old Davie, after his family had recently moved into a new school district. Davie had come home from school on the first afternoon and asked his mother point-blank: 'Mum, what's sex?'

The question smacked her hard. She thought she had two or three years before dealing with that issue and was totally unprepared to field it now. Her racing mind concluded that Davie's new school must be engaged in a liberal sex education programme, and she had no choice but to fill in the details. So, she sat down with her wide-eyed son, and for forty-five minutes gave him a tension-filled harangue about the birds and the bees and the coconut trees.

When she had finished, Davie held up his enrolment card and said, 'Gee, Mum, how am I going to get all that in this tiny little square?'

As Davie's mother discovered, there is a delicate art in knowing when to provide the younger generation with additional information about sex.

One of the most common mistakes committed by some parents and many overzealous educators is the trend towards teaching too much too soon. One parent wrote to me, for example, and said the children in her local junior school were shown films of animals in the act of copulation. That is unwise and dangerous! Available evidence indicates that there are numerous hazards involved in moving too rapidly. Children can sustain a severe emotional jolt by being exposed to realities for which they are not prepared.

Furthermore, it is unwise to place the youngster on an informational timetable that will result in full sophistication too early in life. If eight-year-old children are given an advanced understanding of mature sexual behaviour, it is less likely that they will wait ten or twelve years to apply this knowledge within the confines of marriage.

Another danger resulting from premature instruction involves the threat of overstimulation. Young people can be tantalised by what is taught about the exciting world of grown-up sexual experience. Childhood education should be focused on childish interests, not adult pleasures and desires. I am not implying that sex education should be delayed until childhood has passed. Rather, it seems appropriate that the amount of information youngsters are given should coincide with their social and physical requirement for that awareness.

The child's requests for information provide the best guide to readiness for sex education. Their comments reveal what the youngster thinks about and wants to know. Such questions also offer a natural vehicle for instruction. It is far better for parents to answer these questions at the moment of curiosity than to ignore or evade them, hoping to explain later. Premeditated training sessions often become lengthy, one-way conversations which make both participants uncomfortable.

Although the question-answering approach to sex education is usually superior, the technique is obviously inadequate with children who never ask for information. Some boys and girls are fascinated by sexual reproduction while others never give it a second thought. If a child is uninterested in or doesn't ask about sex, the parent is not relieved of responsibility.

Our two children were opposites at this point. Danae asked all the right (or wrong?) questions one night when she was seven years old. Her shocked mother hadn't expected to have to deal with that subject for a few more years. Shirley stalled for time and came to share the situation with me as I sat at my desk. We promptly invited Danae to sit down for a conversation. Shirley made some hot chocolate and we talked for an hour or so. It all went very smoothly.

Ryan, on the other hand, never asked questions about

sex at all. We volunteered bits and pieces of the story as it seemed appropriate and comfortable, but the specific facts were more difficult to convey. Finally, I took my son on a fishing trip . . . just the two of us. Then as we sat there on the bank waiting for the trout to bite, I said, 'It occurs to me, Ryan, that we have never talked much about sex . . . you know, how babies are made and all that. Maybe this would be a good time to discuss it.'

Ryan sat thoughtfully for several minutes without saying anything. I wondered what he was thinking. Then he said, 'What if I don't wanna know?'

I dragged my kid into the world of reproduction and sexuality, kicking and screaming, but I got him there nonetheless. That is a parental responsibility. Even when it is not easy, the job must be done. If you won't accept the task, someone else will . . . someone who may not share your values.

One final comment is important regarding the timing of sex education in the home. Parents should plan to end their formal instructional programme about the time their child enters puberty (the time of rapid sexual development in early adolescence). Puberty usually begins between ten and thirteen for girls and between eleven and fourteen for boys. Once they enter this developmental period, they are typically embarrassed by discussions of sex with their parents. Adolescents usually resent adult intrusion during this time . . . *unless* they raise the topic themselves. In other words, this is an area where teenagers should invite parents into their lives.

I feel that we should respect their wish. We are given ten or twelve years to provide the proper understanding of human sexuality. After that foundation has been constructed, we largely serve as resources to whom our children can turn when the need exists.

That is *not* to say parents should abdicate their responsibility to provide guidance about issues related to sexuality, dating, marriage, and so on, as opportunities present themselves. Again, sensitivity to the feelings of the teenager is paramount. If he or she wishes to talk, by all means welcome the conversation. In other cases, parental guidance may be most effective if offered *indirectly*. Trusted youth workers at church or in a young people's organisation can often break the ice when parents can't.

Assistance from mother nature?

One of the areas where I have changed my perspective radically since 1970 is in recommending the use of animals, especially dogs and cats, to help explain the reproductive process to children. I *still* think a demonstration of birth is enlightening and helpful, but I am now more familiar with and concerned about the overpopulation of pets and what happens to these poor creatures when they don't have homes. In Los Angeles County alone, more than 100,000 dogs are killed every year in pounds and humane societies. Other homeless animals go hungry or are crushed on our roads. Their suffering is our responsibility!

Our family has adopted our last two dogs from this population of strays, and they have made wonderful pets. Little Mitzi, our present dog, was just hours away from death when we selected her at the pound. But as a lifelong dog lover, I have to tell you the selection process was a difficult experience for us. There in the plastic cages were hundreds of pitiful dogs and cats in need of adoption. Most were traumatised by their circumstances, having been lost or dumped by their owners.

As we strolled between the cages, dogs barked and thrust their paws through the wire to get our attention. Danae put her hand in one cage to pet a lonely pup, who immediately pressed his head into her palm and closed his eyes. I'm sure he did not survive the week. I'll never forget a big brown dog with a hoarse voice who was staring at the doorway when we arrived. He was looking intently at us and yet did not seem to see. Even when we stood in front of his cage, he never took his eyes off the door. Every now and then he would emit a throaty bark that seemed to end in a question mark. Danae then read the identifying card above the cage indicating how he came to be picked up. This dog had been brought in by his owners, and he was intently watching for their return. Obviously, we were not the folks he had in mind.

Perhaps you can understand why Danae and I were looking for the most needy animal we could find. The cute, healthy puppies and kittens had a chance of being adopted, at least. We wanted to give a home to a dog that was certain to be put down. Danae finally called me on a Saturday afternoon to tell me that she had found a good candidate.

I drove to the shelter and quickly agreed with her selection. There, huddled at the back of a cage was a twelve-week-old pup in a terrible condition. She was in a state of semi-starvation, having been picked up on the streets a few days earlier. Her jaw had been broken, perhaps by a fierce kick, and someone had put three stitches in her lip.

We learned later she had pneumonia, round worms, tape worms, and who knows what other problems. She trembled as we approached her cage, but did not rise.

I asked the attendant to let the dog out, and he handed her to me. It was an instant friendship. She nuzzled my hand and looked up as if to say, 'I'm really in a mess, aren't I?' We were hooked.

We left to talk over the matter, but couldn't forget that gentle nuzzle from so helpless a creature. Danae went back and got the dog.

I wish you could see Mitzi today. She is fat, healthy and deliriously happy. When I get home at night, she romps to the front door like a buffalo in stampede. It is as though she knows we rescued her from a living death. And surprisingly, except for a crooked mouth, she looks very much like our previous dog. So Shirley and I no longer have an empty nest at home.

Forgive this diversion from our theme, but it does relate to my earlier recommendation that animals be used to teach the miracle of reproduction and birth. Now I advise parents to have their pets spayed and neutered to prevent the continued problem with overpopulation. If puppies or kittens are desired, be sure to have good homes for them before bringing them into the world.

And if you want to befriend a lonely animal who sits today in a cage just hoping you'll give him a home, head on down to the animal shelter in your area. Neither you nor your kids will ever forget it.

(To all the animal lovers out there who've been cross with me for more than two decades for what I wrote about pet reproduction in *Dare to Discipline*—am I forgiven?)

Conclusion

In the first chapters of this book I discussed the importance of the child's respect for his parents. His attitude towards their leadership is critical to his acceptance of their values and philosophy, including their concept of premarital sexual behaviour. Likewise, the most fundamental element in teaching morality can be achieved through a healthy parent-child relationship during the early years. The obvious hope is that the adolescent will respect and appreciate his parents enough to believe what they say and accept what they recommend.

Unfortunately, however, this loyalty to parents is often an insufficient source of motivation. It is my firm conviction that children should also be taught ultimate loyalty to God. We should make it clear that the merciful God of love whom we serve is also a God of justice. If we choose to defy his moral laws we will suffer certain consequences. God's spiritual imperatives are as inflexible as his physical laws. Those who defy those physical laws will not long survive. Likewise, the wilful violation of God's commandments is equally disastrous, for 'the wages of sin is death'. An adolescent who understands this truth is more likely to live a moral life in the midst of an immoral society.

One further comment may be relevant. Many years ago on my daughter's tenth birthday, Shirley and I gave her a small, gold key. It was attached to a chain worn around her neck, and represented the key to her heart. Through the years, she has kept her vow to give that key to one man only—the one who will share her love through the remainder of her life. You might consider a similar gift for your daughter, or a special ring for your son. These go with them when you're not there and provide a tangible reminder of the lasting, precious gift of sexual fulfilment that God intends for his children.

Q *Your comments about sexually transmitted disease are very unsettling to me. I have three teenagers and am afraid they don't understand how diseases are transmitted and what they can do to the body. That is a very scary subject.*

A Like you, I wonder what it will take to awaken our young people. I interviewed Dr C. Everett Koop while he was Surgeon General of the United States in the mideighties. He said then, 'The AIDS epidemic will soon change the behaviour of everyone. When infected young people begin dying around us, others will be afraid to even kiss anyone.'

That has not occurred as of this writing, even though young people are indeed dying as Dr Koop predicted. The following article, written by reporter Kim Painter, appeared in *USA Today,* 13 April 1992:

AIDS Surging among Teens

AIDS cases among teens and young adults grew 77 per cent in the past two years.

And the 9,000 cases among 13- to 24-year-olds form just the tip of an iceberg: Thousands more are likely HIV-infected; millions more are at risk, says a report by a House committee on children and families.

The report says federal prevention efforts have been inadequate. It cites evidence that teens are risking infection through sex and drug abuse:

—68 per cent of girls, 86 per cent of boys have sex before age 20; fewer than half report condom use.

—3 million teens get a sexually transmitted disease yearly.

—Nearly 3 per cent of high school seniors have used steroids; 1.3 per cent, heroin. Shared needles can spread HIV.[39]

So why have teenagers not become 'afraid to even kiss anyone', as Dr Koop predicted? Because the natural fear of the deadly HIV has been pacified by the safe-sex nonsense. We have seemingly come up with a way to have our cake and eat it, too. It'll be the first time.

Thank goodness for a few doctors who are sounding the alarm and trying to get the uncensored facts to our children. They don't get much press, but some day they will be vindicated. One of the most vocal of these concerned doctors is my good friend, Dr Joe McIlhaney, an obstetrician-gynaecologist in private practice in Austin, Texas. A frequent *Focus on the Family* broadcast guest, he talked about the fallacy of 'safe sex' on a recent programme.

What you hear mostly from the press is what science is going to do for people who have a sexually transmitted disease (STD), how science is going to come up with a vaccine or treatment for AIDS, how antibiotics will kill gonorrhea and chlamydia. What is not discussed is how these STDs leave women's pelvic structures scarred for life, and they end up infertile or having to do expensive procedures to get pregnant later on.

I could name patient after patient in the twenty-two years I've been in practice where I've had to perform a hysterectomy before a woman had the children she wanted because of Pelvic Inflammatory Disease, which is caused by chlamydia and gonorrhea.

The public announcements about 'safe sex' infuriate me, because what they're saying is that you can safely have sex outside of marriage if you use condoms, and you don't have to worry about getting an STD. The message is a lie. The failure rate of condoms is extremely high, and that's why married people don't use them.

I see the victims of these failures in my office every day. These include victims of chlamydia, probably the most prevalent STD, and of Human Papilloma Virus (HPV), which can cause a lasting irritation of the female organs, as well as cancer of the vulva, vagina and cervix. It is one of the most difficult diseases to treat, and kills more than 4,800 women a year. I also see victims of herpes, which some studies indicate is present in up to 30–40 per cent of single, sexually active people, as well as victims of syphilis, which is at a forty-year high.

Rather than expecting science to solve our problems, Dr McIlhaney said a better solution involves a return to spiritual and moral guidelines that have been with us for thousands of years. He concluded:

The people who made my automobile know how it works best and what I need to do to avoid car problems. They tell me that in my Ford manual. Likewise, God knows how we work best, and gave us an 'owner's manual' for the human race: the Bible. In it, he tells us not to have sex until we are married; not to have sex with anybody other than the one man/one woman to whom we are married; and to stay married for the rest of our lives. That's the one and only prescription for safe sex.[40]

Q *Should a child be allowed to 'decide for himself' on matters related to God? Aren't we forcing our religion down our children's throats when we tell them what to believe?*

A Let me answer with an illustration from nature. A little gosling (baby goose) has a peculiar characteristic that is relevan it this point. Shortly after it hatches from its shell it becomes attached, or 'imprinted', to the first thing seen moving nearby. From that time forward, the gosling follows that particular object when it moves in the vicinity. Ordinarily, it becomes imprinted to the mother goose which hatched the new generation.

If she is removed, however, the gosling settles for any mobile substitute, whether alive or not. In fact, a gosling becomes imprinted most easily to a blue football bladder, dragged by on a string. A week later, the baby falls in line behind the bladder as it scoots by.

Time is the critical factor in this process. The gosling is vulnerable to imprinting for only a few seconds after hatching from the shell. If that opportunity is lost, it cannot be regained. In other words, there is a critical, brief period in the gosling's life when this instinctual learning is possible.

There is also a critical period when certain kinds of instruction are easier in the life of children. Although humans have no instincts (only drives, reflexes, urges and so on), there is a brief period during childhood when youngsters are vulnerable to religious training. Their concepts of right and wrong are formulated during this time, and their view of God begins to solidify.

As in the case of the gosling, the opportunity of that period must be seized when it is available. Leaders of the Catholic Church have been widely quoted as saying, 'Give us the child until he is seven years old and we'll have him for life.' They are usually correct, because permanent attitudes can be instilled during these seven vulnerable years.

Unfortunately, however, the opposite is also true. The absence or misapplication of instruction through that prime time period may place a severe limitation on the depth of the child's later devotion to God. When parents withhold indoctrination from their small children, allowing them to 'decide for themselves', the adults are almost guaranteeing that their youngsters will 'decide' in the negative. If parents want their children to have a meaningful faith, they must give up any misguided attempts at objectivity. Children listen closely to discover just how much their parents believe what they preach. Any indecision or ethical confusion from the parent is likely to be magnified in the child.

After the middle adolescent age (ending at about fifteen years), children resent being told exactly what to believe. They don't want religion 'forced down their throat', and should be given more autonomy in what they believe. If the early exposure has been properly conducted, children will have an inner mainstay to steady them. Their early indoctrination, then, is the key to the spiritual attitudes they carry into adulthood.

Q *My young daughter recently told me that she is two months pregnant. What should be my attitude to her now?*

A You cannot reverse the circumstances by being harsh or unloving at this point. Your daughter needs more understanding now than ever before, and you should give it to her if possible. Help her grope through this difficulty and avoid 'I told you so' comments. Many important decisions will face her in the next few months and she will need cool, rational parents to assist in determining the best path to take. Remember, lasting love and affection often develop between people who have survived a crisis together.

Q *When do children begin to develop a sexual nature? Does this occur suddenly during puberty?*

A No, it occurs long before puberty. Perhaps the most important understanding suggested by Freud was his observation that children are not asexual. He stated that sexual gratification begins in the cradle and is first associated with feeding. Behaviour during childhood is influenced considerably by sexual curiosity and interest, although the happy hormones do not take full charge until early adolescence. Thus, it is not uncommon for a four-year-old to be interested in nudity and the sexual apparatus of boys versus girls.

This is an important time in the forming of sexual attitudes. Parents should be careful not to express shock and extreme disapproval of this kind of curiosity. It is believed that many sexual problems begin as a result of inappropriate training during early childhood.

Q *Some colleges and universities permit men and women to live in mixed halls of residence. Others allow unrestricted visiting hours by members of the opposite sex. Do you think this promotes more healthy attitudes towards sex?*

A It certainly promotes more sex, and some people think that's healthy. The advocates of cohabitation try to tell us that young men and women can live together without doing what comes naturally. That is nonsense. The sex drive is one of the strongest forces in human nature, and Joe College is notoriously weak in suppressing it. I would prefer that supporters of mixed halls of residence admit that morality is not very important to them. If abstinence is something we value, then we should at least give it a wobbly-legged chance to survive.

Q *You have said on several occasions that a society can be no more stable than the strengths of its individual family units. More specifically, you said sexual behaviour is directly linked to the survival of nations. Explain how.*

A A book could be written on that topic, but let me give you a short answer to it. This linkage you referred to was first illuminated by J. D. Unwin, a British social anthropologist who spent seven years studying the births and deaths of eighty civilisations. He reported from his exhaustive research that every known culture in the world's history has followed the same sexual pattern: during its early days of existence, pre-marital and extra-marital sexual relationships were strictly prohibited. Great creative energy was associated with this inhibition of sexual expression, causing the culture to prosper. Much later in the life of the society, its people began to rebel against the strict prohibitions, demanding the freedom to release their internal passions. As the mores weakened, the social energy abated, eventually resulting in the decay or destruction of the civilisation.

Dr Unwin stated that the energy which holds a society together is sexual in nature. When a man is devoted to one woman and one family, he is motivated to build, save, protect, plan, and prosper on their behalf. However, when his sexual interests are dispersed and generalised, his effort is invested in the gratification of sensual desires. Dr Unwin concluded: 'Any human society is free either to display great energy, or to enjoy sexual freedom; the evidence is that they cannot do both for more than one generation.'

It is my belief that the worsening economic situation in the Western world and the difficulties families and children are experiencing can be traced to our departure from traditional values and biblical concepts of morality.

Q *You spoke of kindness to animals. That reminds me to ask you about my seven-year-old son who is cruel to animals. We've caught him doing some pretty awful things to dogs and cats in our neighbourhood. Of course, we punished him, but I wonder if there is anything to be more concerned about here?*

A I would consider cruelty to animals as a serious symptom to be evaluated by a professional. Children who do such things are not typically just going through a phase. It should be seen as a warning sign of a possible psychological problem that could be rather persistent. It also appears to be associated with sexual abuse in childhood. I don't want to alarm you or overstate the case, but adults committed to a life of violent crime were often cruel to animals in their childhood. This fact was verified in a recent study by the American Humane Association.[41] I suggest that you take your son to a psychologist or other behavioural specialist who can evaluate his mental health. And by all means, do not tolerate unkindness to animals.

Q *Is AIDS God's plague sent to punish homosexuals, lesbians and other promiscuous people?*

A I would think not, because little babies and others who bear no responsibility are suffering. But consider this: if I choose to leap off a ten-storey building, I will die when my body hits the ground below. It's inevitable. But gravity was not designed by God to punish my folly. He established physical laws that can be violated only at great peril. So it is with his moral laws. They are as real and predictable as the principles that govern the physical universe. Thus, we knew (and he *certainly* knew) with the onset of the sexual revolution back in the sixties that this day of disease and promiscuity would come. It is here, and what we do with our situation will determine how much we and our children will suffer in the future.

By the way, did you know that God created the moral basis for the universe *before* he made the heavens and the earth? His concept of right and wrong was not an afterthought that came along with the Ten Commandments. No, it was an expression of God's divine nature and was in force before 'the beginning'.

That's what we read in Proverbs 8:22–36, referring to the universal moral law in the first person:

The Lord brought me forth as the first of his works, before his deeds of old; I was appointed from eternity, from the beginning, before the world began. When there were no oceans, I was given birth, when there were no springs abounding with water; before the mountains were settled in place, before the hills, I was given birth, before he made the earth or its fields or any of the dust of the world. I was there when he set the heavens in place, when he marked out the horizon on the face of the deep, when he established the clouds above and fixed securely the fountains of the deep, when he gave the sea its boundary so the waters would not overstep his command, and when he marked out the foundations of the earth. Then I was the craftsman at his side. I was filled with delight day after day, rejoicing always in his presence, rejoicing in his whole world and delighting in mankind. Now then, my sons, listen to me; blessed are those who keep my ways. Listen to my instruction and be wise; do not ignore it. Blessed is the man who listens to me, watching daily at my doors, waiting at my doorway. For whoever finds me finds life and receives favour from the Lord. But whoever fails to find me harms himself; all who hate me love death (NIV).

These last two verses say it all. If we conform our behaviour to God's ancient moral prescription, we are entitled to the sweet benefits of life itself. But if we defy its clear imperatives, then death is the inevitable consequence. AIDS is only one avenue by which sickness and death befall those who play Russian roulette with God's moral law.

11

A Moment for Mum

As the previous chapters have indicated, the responsibilities of effective parenthood are staggeringly heavy at times. Children place great demands on their guardians, as a colleague of mine discovered one morning when he said good-bye to his three-year-old daughter.

'I have to go to work, now,' he said.

'That's all right, Daddy. I'll forgive you,' she tearfully replied. She was willing to overlook his insult just once, but she didn't want him to let it happen again. As this little girl demonstrated, children are terribly dependent on their parents and the task of meeting their needs is a full-time job.

Some of them are much more aware of the power struggle with their parents than Mum and Dad appear to be. That fact was illustrated numerous times after the original publication of *Dare to Discipline*. Some children who couldn't even read knew there was stuff in that book that helped their parents control them. One youngster went to a bookshelf, pulled this publication out from among hundreds, and proceeded to throw it in the fire. Others were even more explicit about how they felt.

The mother of a very strong-willed three-year-old shared a story with me that made me smile. This youngster named Laura had managed to wind the entire family around her little finger. She was out of control and seemed to be enjoying it. Both the mother and father were exasperated in trying to deal with their little spitfire— until, that is, Mum happened to be in a book shop and stumbled across *Dare to Discipline*. She bought a copy and soon learned, at least according to the opinion of its author, that it is appropriate under certain circumstances to spank a child. Thus, the next time Laura played her defiant games, she got a shocking surprise on her little backside.

Laura was a very bright child and she was able to work out where her mum had got that idea. Believe it or not, the mother came in the next morning and found her copy of *Dare to Discipline* floating in the toilet.

That may be the most graphic editorial comment anyone has made about my writings. I'm told Dr Benjamin Spock is loved by millions of children who are being brought up according to his philosophy. I have an entire generation that would like to catch me in a blind alley. But I'm also convinced that some young adults who have grown up on love and discipline in balance are now bringing up *their* children that way. It is still true today, as it was when they were tots, that a child will be ruled by the rudder or the rock. Some things never change.

Even with a clear game plan in mind, however, bringing up children properly is one of life's richest challenges. It is not uncommon for a mother, particularly, to feel overwhelmed by the complexity of her parental task. In many homes, she is the primary protector for each child's health, education, intellect, personality, character and emotional stability. As such, she must serve as doctor, nurse, psychologist, teacher, minister, cook and policeman. Since in many cases she is with the children longer each day than her husband, she is the chief disciplinarian and main giver of security and love.

The reality is that she and her husband will not know whether or not she is handling these matters properly until it is too late to change her methodology. Furthermore, Mum's responsibilities extend far beyond her children. She must also meet her obligations to her husband, her church, her relatives, her friends and, often, her employer. Each of these areas demands her best effort, and the conscientious mother often finds herself racing through the day in a breathless attempt to be all things to all people.

Most healthy individuals can tolerate encircling pressures as long as each responsibility can be kept under relative control. Hard work and diligence are personally rewarding, provided anxiety and frustration are kept at a minimum. However, much greater self-control is needed when a threatening problem develops in one of the critical areas.

That is, if a child becomes very ill, marital problems erupt, or Mum is unjustly criticised in the neighbourhood, then the other routine tasks become more difficult to accomplish. Certainly, there are occasions in the life of every mother when she looks in the mirror and asks, 'How can I make it through this day?' The simple suggestions in the remaining portion of this book are designed to help her answer that exasperated question.

Reserve some time for yourself

It is important for a mother to put herself on the priority list, too. At least once a week she should play tennis, go shopping, spend time at the gym, or simply 'waste' an occasional afternoon. It is unhealthy for anyone to work all the time, and the entire family will profit from her periodic recreation.

Even more important is the protection and maintenance of romance in her marriage. A husband and wife should have a date every week or two, leaving the children at home and forgetting the day's problems for an evening. If the family's finances seemingly prohibit such activities, I suggest that other expenditure be re-examined. I believe that money spent on togetherness will yield many more benefits than an additional piece of furniture or a newer car. A woman finds life much more enjoyable if she knows she is the sweetheart, and not just the wife, of her husband.

Don't struggle with things you can't change

The first principle of mental health is to learn to accept the inevitable. To do otherwise is to run with the brakes on. Too many people make themselves unhappy over insignificant irritants which should be ignored. In these cases, contentment is no more stable than the weakest link in the chain of circumstances surrounding their lives. All but one of the conditions in a particular woman's life might be perfect: she has good health, a devoted husband, happy children, plenty of food, warmth and shelter, and a personal challenge. Nevertheless, she might be miserable because she doesn't like her mother-in-law. This one negative element can be allowed to overshadow all the good fortune surrounding her.

Life has enough crises in it without magnifying our troubles during good times, yet peace of mind is often surrendered for such insignificant causes. I wonder how many women are discontented today because they don't have something which either wasn't invented or wasn't fashionable just fifty years ago. Men and women should recognise that dissatisfaction with life can become nothing more than a bad habit—a costly attitude that can rob them of life's pleasures.

Don't deal with big problems late at night

Fatigue does strange things to human perception. After a hard day, the most simple tasks may appear insurmountable. All problems seem more unsolvable at night, and the decisions that are reached then may be more emotional than rational. When couples discuss finances or other family problems in the wee hours, they are asking for trouble. Their tolerance to frustration is low, often leading to fights which should never have occurred. Tension and hostility can be avoided by simply delaying important topics until morning. A good night's sleep and a rich cup of coffee can go a long way towards defusing the problem.

Try making a list

When the work load gets particularly heavy there is comfort to be found in making a list of the duties to be performed. The advantages of writing down one's responsibilities are threefold: (a) You know you won't forget anything; (b) You guarantee that the most important jobs will get done first. Thus, if you don't get finished by the end of the day, you will have at least done the items that were most critical; (c) You leave a record of accomplishments by crossing tasks off the list as they are completed.

Seek divine assistance

The concepts of marriage and parenthood were not human inventions. God, in his infinite wisdom, created and ordained the family as the basic unit of procreation and companionship. The solutions to the problem of modern parenthood can be found through the power of prayer and personal appeal to the Creator. Indeed, I believe parents should commit themselves to *daily* prayer and supplication on behalf of their children. The task is too frightening on our own, and there is not enough knowledge in the books (including this one) to guarantee the outcome of our parenting duties. We desperately need divine help with the job!

The principles of discipline which I have summarised in this book can hardly be considered new ideas. Most of these recommendations were first written in the Scriptures, dating back at least 2,000 years to biblical times. Consider the clarity with which the following verses outline a healthy parental attitude towards children and vice versa.

> He [the father] must have proper authority in his own household, and be able to control and command the respect of his children. (For if a man cannot rule in his own house how can he look after the Church of God?) (1 Tim 3:4–5, PHILLIPS).

This verse acknowledges the fact that respect must be 'commanded'. It is not a byproduct of human nature, but it is inherently related to control and discipline.

> My son, do not regard lightly the discipline of the Lord, nor lose courage when you are punished by him. For the Lord disciplines him whom he loves [Note: Discipline and love work hand in hand; one is a function of the other] and chastises every son whom he receives. It is for discipline that you have to endure. God is treating you as sons; for what son is there whom his father does not discipline? If you are left without discipline, in which all have participated, then you are illegitimate children and not sons. Besides this, we have had earthly fathers to discipline us and we respected them . . . [Note: The relationship between discipline and respect was recognised more than 2,000 years ago] For the moment all discipline seems painful rather than pleasant; later it yields the peaceful fruit of righteousness to those who have been trained by it (Heb 12:5–9, 11, RSV).

The purpose of this scripture is to demonstrate that the parent's relationship with his child should be modelled after God's relationship with man. In its ultimate beauty, that interaction is characterised by abundant love—a love unparalleled in tenderness and mercy. This same love leads the benevolent father to guide, correct, and even bring some pain to the child when it is necessary for his eventual good. I find it difficult to comprehend how this message has been so thoroughly misunderstood during the past twenty years.

> Children, the right thing for you to do is to obey your parents as those whom God has set over you. The first commandment to contain a promise was: 'Honour thy father and thy mother that it may be well with thee, and that thou mayest

live long on the earth.' Fathers, don't over-correct your children or make it difficult for them to obey the commandment. Bring them up with Christian teaching in Christian discipline (Eph 6:1–4, PHILLIPS).

Foolishness is bound in the heart of a child; but the rod of correction shall drive it far from him (Prov 22:15, KJV).

This recommendation has troubled some people, leading them to claim that the 'rod' was not a paddle, but a measuring stick with which to evaluate the child. The following passage was included expressly for those who were confused on that point.

Withhold not correction from the child; for if thou beatest him with the rod, he shall not die. Thou shalt beat him with the rod, and shalt deliver his soul from hell (Prov 23:13–14, KJV).

Certainly, if the 'rod' is a measuring stick, you now know what to do with it! (Note: Please don't grill me on this. I would ask that you heed all of my disclaimers related to child abuse, which I expressed in earlier chapters.)

He that spareth his rod hateth his son; but he that loveth him chasteneth him betimes (Prov 13:24, KJV).

The rod and reproof give wisdom; but a child left to himself bringeth his mother to shame (Prov 29:15, KJV).

Correct thy son, and he shall give thee rest; yea, he shall give delight unto thy soul (Prov 29:17, KJV).

From Genesis to Revelation, there is consistent foundation on which to build an effective philosophy of parent-child relationships. It is my belief that we have departed from the standard which was clearly outlined in both the Old and New Testaments, and that deviation is costing us a heavy toll in the form of social turmoil. Self-control, human kindness, respect and peacefulness can again be manifest if we will *dare to discipline* in our homes and schools.

Let me leave you, now, with a wonderful old poem written by Alice Pearson. It focuses on *the* most vital responsibility in parenting—that of introducing our children to Jesus Christ and getting them safely through this dangerous and turbulent world. That should be, after all, the ultimate goal for every believing parent the world over.

Are All the Children In?

I think oftimes as night draws nigh,
Of an old house on the hill,
And of a yard all wide
And blossom-starred
Where the children played at will.
And when the night at last came down
Hushing the merry din,
Mother would look around and ask,
'Are all the children in?'

Oh, it's many and many a year since then,
And the old house on the hill
No longer echoes to childish feet,
And the yard is still, so still.
But I see it all as the shadows creep,
And though many the years have been since then,
I can hear mother ask,
'Are all the children in?'

I wonder if when the shadows fall
On the last short earthly day;
When we say goodbye to the world outside
All tired with our childish play;
When we step out into the other land
Where mother so long has been,
Will we hear her ask,
Just as of old,
'Are all the children in?'[1]

Notes

Chapter 1. The Challenge

[1] Luther Woodward, with Morton Edwards (ed), *Your Child from Two to Five* (Permabooks: New York, 1955).

[2] James C. Dobson, *The Strong-Willed Child* (Tyndale House Publishers, Inc: Wheaton, 1978), p 55. (Published in the UK by Kingsway: Eastbourne, 1978.)

[3] John B. Watson and R. R. Watson, *Psychological Care of Infant and Child* (Norton & Company, 1928), pp 81–82, 87.

Chapter 4. Questions and Answers

[1] James Dobson, *The Strong-Willed Child* (Tyndale House Publishers, Inc: Wheaton, 1978), p 52. (Published in the UK by Kingsway: Eastbourne, 1978.)

Chapter 5. The Miracle Tools, Part 1

[1] James Dobson, *Hide or Seek* (Fleming H. Revell Company: Old Tappan, NJ, 1974), p 69. (Published in the UK by Hodder & Stoughton.)

Chapter 6. The Miracle Tools, Part 2

1 James Dobson, *The Strong-Willed Child* (Tyndale House Publishers, Inc: Wheaton, 1978), p 136. (Published in the UK by Kingsway: Eastbourne, 1978.)

Chapter 7. Discipline in Learning

1 Sheldon Glueck and Eleanor T. Glueck, *Unraveling Juvenile Delinquency* (Commonwealth Fund, 1950).

Chapter 8. The Barriers to Learning, Part 1

1 Sources include the following:
Brian D. Ray, 'A nationwide study of home education: Family characteristics, legal matters, and student achievement' (1990, available from the National Home Education Research Institute, c/o Western Baptist College, 5000 Deer Park Drive SE, Salem, OR 97301, USA).
Brian D. Ray, 'Home education in North Dakota: Family characteristics and student achievement' (1991, available from the National Home Education Research Institute).
Brian D. Ray, 'Home education in Oklahoma: Family characteristics, student achievement, and policy matters' (1991, available from the National Home Education Research Institute).

2 Sources include the following:
Brian D. Ray, 'A nationwide study of home education: Family characteristics, legal matters, and student achievement' (1990, available from the National Home Education Research Institute, c/o Western Baptist College, 5000 Deer Park Drive SE, Salem, OR 97301, USA).
Sue S. Greene, 'Home study in Alaska: A profile of K-12 students in the Alaska Centralized Correspondence Study

Program' (ERIC Document Reproduction Service No ED 255 494).

Brian D. Ray, and Jon Wartes, 'The academic achievement and affective development of home-schooled children', *Home Schooling: Political, Historical and Pedagogical Perspectives* (Ablex Publishing Corporation: Norwood, NJ, 1991).

Jennie F. Rakestraw, 'Home Schooling in Alabama', *Home School Researcher,* 4(4) (1988): pp 1–6.

Jon Wartes, 'Five years of home-school testing within Washington state' (December 1991, available from the Washington Home School Research Project at 15109 NE 169 Pl, Woodinville, WA, 98072 USA).

[3] Linda R. Montgomery 'The effect of home schooling on the leadership skills of home-schooled students', *Home School Researcher*, 5(1): pp 1–10.

[4] Sources include the following:

Wilfred Aikin, *The Story of the Eight Year Study*, 4 vols (Harper: New York, 1942).

Mona Maarse Delahooke, 'Home educated children's social/emotional adjustment and academic achievement: A comparative study'. Unpublished doctoral dissertation, California School of Professional Psychology, Los Angeles, CA, USA.

Linda R. Montgomery, 'The effect of home schooling on the leadership skills of home-schooled students', *Home School Researcher*, 5(1): pp 1–10.

[5] James C. Dobson, *The Strong-Willed Child* (Tyndale House Publishers, Inc: Wheaton, 1978), pp 158–160. (Published in the UK by Kingsway: Eastbourne, 1978.)

Chapter 9. The Barriers to Learning, Part 2

[1] Mona Behan, 'What Do You Say to a C?', *Parenting Magazine* (April 1992): p 47.

2 James C. Dobson, *The Strong-Willed Child* (Tyndale House Publishers, Inc: Wheaton, 1978), pp 158–160. (Published in the UK by Kingsway: Eastbourne, 1978.)

Chapter 10. Discipline in Morality

1 Gabriel Escobar, 'Slayings in Washington Hit New High, 436, for 3rd year', *Washington Post* (24 November 1990).

2 Steven Manning, 'A National Emergency', *Scholastic Update* (5 April 1991): p 2.

3 Gordon Witkin, 'Kids Who Kill', *U.S. News & World Report* (8 April 1991): p 27.

4 'Alcohol Use and Abuse in America', *Gallup Report,* no 265 (October 1987): p 3.

5 Barbara R. Lorch and Robert H. Hughes, 'Church Youth, Alcohol and Drug Education Programs, and Youth Substance Use', *Journal of Alcohol and Drug Education,* vol 33, no 2 (Winter 1988): p 15.

6 *Guidelines for Comprehensive Sexuality Education* (National Guidelines Task Force, Sex Information and Education Council of the US, 1991).

7 Pamela McDonnell, Sexually Transmitted Diseases Division, Centers for Disease Control, US Dept of Health & Human Services, 16 March 1992.

8 Scott W. Wright, '1 in 100 tested at UT has AIDS virus', *Austin American Statesman* (14 July 1991): p A14. The federally funded study was based on a non-random sample.

9 'Heterosexual HIV Transmission Up in the United States', *American Medical News* (3 February 1992): p 35.

10 US Dept of Health & Human Services, Public Health Service, Centers for Disease Control, 1991 Division of STD/HIV Prevention *Annual Report*, p 13.

11 Health & Human Services *Annual Report*, p 13.

12 McDonnell, *op cit.*

13 Health & Human Services *Annual Report*, p 13.

14 *Ibid.*

15 *Ibid.*

16 Robert E. Johnson et al, 'A Seroepidemiologic Survey of the Prevalence of Herpes Simplex Virus Type 2 Infection in the United States', *New England Journal of Medicine*, vol 321 (6 July 1989): pp 7–12.

17 Health & Human Services *Annual Report*, p 13.

18 C. Kuehn and F. Judson, 'How common are sexually transmitted infections in adolescents?', *Clinical Practice Sexuality* 5 (1989): pp 19–25; as cited by Sandra D. Gottwald et al, 'Profile: Adolescent Ob/Gyn Patients at the University of Michigan, 1989', *The American Journal of Gynecologic Health*, vol 5 (May/June 1991): p 23.

19 Kay Stone, Sexually Transmitted Diseases Division, Centers for Disease Control, US Dept of Health & Human Services, 20 March 1992.

20 Elise F. Jones and Jacqueline Darroch Forrest, 'Contraceptive Failure in the United States: Revised Estimates from the 1982 National Survey of Family Growth', *Family Planning Perspectives*, vol 21 (May/June 1989): p 103.

21 *Ibid*, p 105.

22 Lode Wigersma and Ron Oud, 'Safety and Acceptability of Condoms for Use by Homosexual Men as a Prophylactic Against Transmission of HIV during Anogenital Sexual Intercourse', *British Medical Journal* 295 (11 July 1987): p 94.

23 Marcia F. Goldsmith, 'Sex in the Age of AIDS Calls for Common Sense and Condom Sense', *Journal of the American Medical Association* 257 (1 May 1987): p 2262.

24 Susan G. Arnold et al, 'Latex Gloves Not Enough to Exclude Viruses', *Nature*, vol 335 (1 September 1988): p 19.

25 Nancy E. Dirubbo, 'The Condom Barrier', *American Journal of Nursing* (October 1987): p 1306.

[26] Theresa Crenshaw, from remarks made at the National Conference on HIV, Washington, DC, 15–18 November 1991.

[27] 'Condom Roulette', *Washington Watch*, vol 3 (Family Research Council: Washington, January 1992): p 1.

[28] William D. Mosher and James W. McNally, 'Contraceptive Use at First Premarital Intercourse: United States, 1965–1988', *Family Planning Perspectives*, vol 23 (May/June 1991): p 111.

[29] Cheryl D. Hayes (ed), *Risking the Future: Adolescent Sexuality, Pregnancy and Childbearing* (National Academy Press: Washington 1987), pp 46–49.

[30] Planned Parenthood poll, 'American Teens Speak: Sex, Myths, TV and Birth Control' (Louis Harris & Associates, Inc: New York, 1986), p 24.

[31] 'Condom Roulette', *In Focus*, vol 25 (Family Research Council: Washington, February 1992), p 2.

[32] Gilbert L. Crouse, Office of Planning and Evaluation, US Dept of Health & Human Services, 12 March 1992, based on data from Planned Parenthood's Alan Guttmacher Institute. Increase calculated from 1973, first year of legal abortion.

[33] US Congress, House Committee on Energy and Commerce, Subcommittee on Health and the Environment, 'The Reauthorization of Title X of the Public Health Service Act' (testimony submitted by Charmaine Yoest), 102nd Congress, 2nd session, 19 March 1991, p 2.

[34] Margaret A. Fischl et al, 'Heterosexual Transmission of Human Immunodeficiency Virus (HIV): Relationship of Sexual Practices to Seroconversion', III International Conference on AIDS, 1–5 June 1987, Abstracts Volume, p 178.

[35] US Dept of Health & Human Services, National Centers for Health Statistics, Centers for Disease Control, 'Percent of

Women 15–19 Years of Age Who Are Sexually Experienced, by Race, Age and Marital Status: United States, 1988', National Survey of Family Growth.

36 Joseph S. McIlhaney, Jr, *Sexuality and Sexually Transmitted Diseases* (Baker Book House: Grand Rapids, 1990), p 137.

37 A.M.B. Goldstein and Susan M. Garabedian-Ruffalo, 'A Treatment Update to Resistant Gonorrhea', *Medical Aspects of Human Sexuality* (August 1991): p 39.

38 Reprinted with permission by Word Publishing. James C. Dobson and Gary L. Bauer, *Children at Risk* (Word Publishing: Dallas, 1990), pp 11–13.

39 Reprinted with permission by *USA Today*. Kim Painter, 'AIDS Surging Among Teens', *USA Today* (13 April 1992).

40 Joe McIlhaney, 'A Doctor Speaks Out on Sexually Transmitted Diseases' (Focus on the Family: Colorado Springs).

41 S.R. Kellert and A.R. Felthouse, 'Childhood cruelty toward animals among criminals and noncriminals', *Human Relations*, vol 38, (1985): pp 1113–1129. Also, A.R. Felthouse and S.R. Kellert, 'Childhood cruelty to animals and later aggression against people: A review', *American Journal of Psychiatry* (1987): pp 144, 710–717.

Chapter 11. A Moment for Mum

1 Reprinted with permission by Randall Pearson. Alice Pearson, 'Are All the Children In?', *Heartspun and Homespun Poems* (Adventure Publications, 1982).

Books by Dr James Dobson

● *The New Dare to Discipline* – New generations of parents and teachers continue to face the timeless challenge of helping children to grow into mature and responsible adults. This book will inspire and equip all those who wish to bring up and teach children in an environment of encouragement and loving discipline.

● *The Strong-Willed Child* – Children are costly in time and effort, as well as financially – but they are certainly worth the price. This book shows us how to cope with the difficulties and how to train the child who is strong-willed and assertive.

● *Preparing for Adolescence* – Young people between the ages of nine and fifteen are invited to read these pages and so face the upheaval of adolescence with their eyes open. Here they will find information, advice and encouragement.

● *Man to Man About Women* – This book is for men and women – written by a man for men, but its aim is to understand one of God's greatest gifts to man – a woman! He covers several key areas of a woman's life and personality, including self-esteem, depression, romance, sex and children.

● *Love Must Be Tough* – In the light of the distressing growth of marital breakdown and divorce, James Dobson writes for all those who are experiencing a crisis in their marriage. All those in relationships where human interests can collide need to consider the practical wisdom contained in this book.

All the above are available from Kingsway Publications

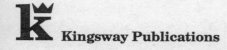

Kingsway Publications